Physical Education

PHYSICAL EDUCATION

The Behavior Modification Approach
By Robert J. Presbie
Paul L. Brown

The Curriculum Series

National Education Association
Washington, D.C.

Stock No. 2101-0 (paper)
        2102-9 (cloth)

Library of Congress Cataloging in Publication Data

Presbie, Robert J
    Physical education.

    Bibliography: p.
    1. Physical education and training. 2. Be-
havior modification. I. Brown, Paul L., 1942-
joint author. II. Title.
GV363.P73   613.7'07   76-51370
ISBN 0-8106-2102-9
ISBN 0-8106-2101-0 pbk.

Robert J. Presbie and Paul L. Brown are both members of the Department of Psychology at the State University of New York, College at New Paltz. They are the authors of *Behavior Modification* in NEA's What Research Says to the Teacher Series.

CONTENTS

INTRODUCTION

Good physical education is important in the development of the strength, stamina, and physical fitness which contributes to sound health. Good physical education also contributes to the development of the motor skills which individuals need to engage in a variety of games, sports, and leisure time activities successfully. Most would agree that the healthy body and the athletic skills which physical education helps to develop are essential to everyone's education and future well-being. The development of sound health and athletic skills is important not only in its own right, but in other ways as well. Their development directly affects the development of various social skills and the interactions among individuals. Additionally, because more and more leisure time is becoming available to more people, the effective use of recreational activities from a health perspective will become increasingly important in the future. How well this will be accomplished depends directly on the extent to which sound health practices and athletic skills are being taught to individuals while they are still in their formative years in school. The goal of physical education, very clearly then, is to develop lifelong physical-fitness practices and athletic skills, from kindergarten through old age.

But regardless of the best intentions of physical educators and the well-established physical education curricula, many individuals report having had unsuccessful physical education experiences in school. (215) Also, many don't acquire the basic motor skills necessary for common games and sports (157), and many are not as healthy, or physically fit or active, as they should be for their own welfare. (93)

Learning Physical Fitness and Athletic Skills

Although there are gross differences in the physical fitness and athletic abilities of individuals and although there is an alarming proportion of people who are physically inactive, overweight, and in other ways physically unfit, there is every reason to believe that this state of affairs can be substantially improved. This is based on the proposition that physical fitness and athletic skills are to a large part learned behaviors. If this is so, then one should be able to teach effectively both physical fitness and athletic skills to those who are in their formative years. One should also be able to teach effectively people with ineffective or maladaptive physical fitness and athletic behaviors how to unlearn these bad habits and substitute more adaptive ones for them. It is unreasonable to expect to produce Olympic or professional athletes, but there is every reason to believe that the overall physical fitness and athletic skills of most individuals can be improved much beyond what they are now if the appropriate principles of learning are systematically used as teaching procedures in the gym.

That physical education skills are to a large extent learned behaviors may easily make common sense, but it is difficult to appreciate this fact fully unless a more concrete example can be visualized. Visit any high school or college and look at the young men and women there. They vary enormously in the extent to which they are physically fit, have poor posture, possess athletic skills, or are overweight. Then visit one of our military academies and look at the young men and women there. They stand straight, not a one of them is even moderately overweight, and they exhibit very good physical fitness and athletic abilities. These individuals are of course specifically selected for these characteristics initially, but after four years of school, compared to any similar college class, the academy cadets substantially maintain or enhance these characteristics. Their college peers do not. The important difference in the experiences they have during these years is that one group of young men and women is consistently taught certain physical fitness and athletic skills, the other is not. The differences are readily visible.

If physical fitness and athletic skills are to a large extent learned, then the important questions for physical educators to consider are how does one teach these skills to young men and women, and what does one do to get them to continue to develop and maintain these skills throughout their lives? Physical educators taking this approach will thus have to be concerned with finding out which teaching principles (based on behavioral research) can be used to facilitate their curricular goals. They will also have to be concerned with how they can specifically implement these teaching principles as a technology of teaching and as practical teaching procedures in the gymnasium and on the playing fields.

EDUCATIONAL ANALYSES OF TEACHING PRINCIPLES AND PROCEDURES

In order to have a better appreciation of the behavior modification approach to implementing the physical education curriculum, it is necessary first to review briefly past and present educational approaches of improving teaching in the gymnasium. This will allow one to compare some of the similarities and differences of the present approach to the traditional ones. It should also help one to appreciate the potential promise the behavior modification approach has for helping to implement physical education curricula into practice.

Traditional Educational Research in Physical Education

It has been suggested that watching what the teacher does in the gym class—seeing what happens there—will help to uncover the important principles of teaching and teaching procedures which distinguish effective from ineffective physical education teachers. (4) Based upon Flander's Interaction Analysis (67), a number of researchers have developed a variety of different ways of categorizing and recording what goes on between teachers and their students during physical education classes. (19,66,157,159,248) Although this research has yielded a variety of interesting findings, much of this information is merely descriptive and, therefore, not of any immediate practical use to the physical education teacher. Indeed, even with this and other kinds of research information, some physical educators admit that they don't know what good teaching is in physical education (87), while others note that the very nature of the underlying discipline of physical education is not quite clear to the physical education profession itself. (207) In general, teachers haven't been effectively translating available theory and research findings into classroom practice.

The article on "Research on Teaching Physical Education" (157) in the *Second Handbook on Research on Teaching* (233) goes so far as to state that the teaching of physical education has little to do with our present scientific knowledge about learning, and that in practice it has even less to do with our present knowledge about research on teaching. While the importance of research is clearly acknowledged as necessary for improving the teacher's teaching and the student's learning, some individuals suggest that the findings and methodologies of a number of the social sciences, including the discipline of psychology, may not be of any practical benefit to physical educators. (170)

Physical educators are thus faced with a paradoxical state of affairs. On the one hand the importance of research for teaching is stressed by many members of the physical education profession. But on the other hand more than a few physical educators are quite pessimistic about what such a research-oriented approach has yielded in the past, and what it might possibly deliver in the future. What are physical education teachers to do, and where can they look for guidance?

Several other sources of information have been readily available for physical educators to consider in their quest to improve their own teaching procedures and, more importantly, their students' physical fitness and athletic skills. First there are the vast numbers of research studies on motor skills learning. (157,177,212) Unfortunately many of these types of studies are done in laboratory settings where the subjects engage in experiments dealing with motor behaviors which may be quite unrelated to the everyday kinds of physical education skills teachers in schools and colleges have to teach their students. Quite a few other motor learning studies, although they may deal with real-life athletic skills such as tennis

(43), or archery (210) report no significant differences between the experimental and control conditions of their studies. Even those studies which do report significant results in their experiments when dealing with such relevant physical education skills as ball handling (141), standing broad jump (37), or golf (227), may also be limited in use or even useless to physical education teachers. The behavioral principles and teaching procedures are stated neither clearly nor in sufficient detail by their researchers. Furthermore the behavioral principles and procedures are rarely translated into practical concrete procedures which can be immediately used by teachers in their gym classes. Such kinds of highly technical and esoteric studies which produce nonsignificant, insignificant, equivocal, incomprehensible, or untranslatable results are of limited or little help for assisting physical education teachers in translating their curriculums into practice.

A second source readily available to physical education teachers for improving their teaching procedures are the success stories described by coaches and physical education teachers in such journals as *Coaching Clinic, Scholastic Coach, The Athletic Journal,* and other sources. These anecdotal reports related specific things coaches or teachers have done that they considered to have been effective in improving athletic skills and physical fitness. Many of these articles are concerned with such general topics as "motivation" (18,39,92), "personalizing" instruction (56), and making better use of statistics and charts (31,146). Although common sense ideas such as using "positive motivation" (118) or keeping things "simple" (209) are discussed in these and similar articles, they too, just as the more highly technical and esoteric research articles do, leave much to be desired. They don't provide the physical educator with enough information in order to repeat the success of the writers of these articles. These kinds of articles don't tell the reader exactly what behavioral principles were used to improve the athletic skills of the individuals involved in these success stories.

These kinds of success stories try to convey tricks of the trade. Several of them even refer to the teaching/coaching procedures they used as "gimmicks" (148,168), while others refer to such advice as teaching "hints." (157) What they present to the reader is a bag of tricks. But there is no doubt that these tricks work in many instances as the authors of these kinds of articles invariably report that their teams win more often, and that their athletes improve their individual performances substantially. As one of these writers put it, "It would appear that we must be doing something right." (148:74) Indeed, they are doing something right, but exactly what is it that they are doing? Because they don't reveal the technicalities of their tricks of the trade, the underlying behavioral principles and teaching procedures they used aren't defined or communicated to those who might directly benefit from knowing about them. So whether the suggestions physical education teachers get come from various kinds of direct observations of their teaching, laboratory type research, or advice from successful coaches and teachers, they are still faced with the problem of making these suggestions directly relevant to their everyday teaching in their gym classes.

Making Physical Education Research Relevant

Recently there has been an increasing concern for objectifying physical education teaching (4,75), for being more generally accountable (64,211), and more specifically accountable in terms of the behavioral outcomes reflected in the improved behaviors of students in physical education classes. (170) The AAHPER Physical Education Division position papers for both the elementary (2) and the secondary school programs (108) reflected these concerns in their common emphasis on sequentially presenting clear-cut behavioral objectives to students and continually evaluating each student's progress with respect to these behavioral objectives. The rationale behind these suggested changes in educational practices is that they should make teachers more efficient and effective, and that this will be reflected in an increased proficiency in their students. It has also been argued that such changes should help to change the poor image physical education has among some members of the public, school administrators, and students. Physical education's image should improve directly as teaching procedures and behavioral outcomes are made more objective and public. (205)

The underlying nature of these suggestions for improving physical education teaching revolves around the search for a more scientific analysis of what is going on between the physical education teacher and his or her students, and how one can effectively use the results of such research studies as teaching procedures for the gym class in a practical and concrete fashion. If this kind of a search is successful, it should result in the development of teaching and evaluation procedures which will indeed be practical, concrete, objective, accountable, and, most importantly, effective. The results of such work should also have the positive side effect of providing teachers, educational administrators, even parents and students themselves, with the opportunity to recognize observable changes in students' behaviors that can be seen as sequential steps in the process of improving physical fitness and athletic skills.

So what is needed in physical education is more applied research—not just any kind of applied research but, rather, applied research which can be immediately and directly used in the gym. (216) Physical education teachers need scientifically demonstrated practical teaching procédures which they can use with their existing physical education curriculum guides (46,50, 202,235) or with their own curricula. Once they develop such teaching tools, they can then begin to translate their curricula more successfully into practice.

THE BEHAVIOR MODIFICATION APPROACH IN PHYSICAL EDUCATION

The last decade has seen the development of a scientifically oriented applied-research approach which has been demonstrated to be very practical, objective, and accountable in many different areas of application (44,106,121), including psychiatry (3); psychological work in institutions with schizophrenic adults (5, 195); autistic and retarded individuals (229,242); delinquents (223); social work (65,225); nursing, physical therapy, and medicine (99,120,191); parent training (12,113,142); business, industry, and management (27,128); and even in the personal self-control of one's own behaviors such as smoking, overeating, nail biting, etc. (241,246) This kind of work is not of any limited or regional nature; it is international. (228) Extensive successful applications have also been demonstrated in many different aspects of education (29,47,156,178,180,230), from nursery school (2,25), through elementary school (81,130), high school (24,144), and college. (28,48,49,241,246)

This practical, applied approach to dealing with educational and virtually any kind of behavioral concerns also offers physical education teachers similar kinds of concrete, practical, and effective procedures to use in studying and improving their students' behaviors (and their own teaching behaviors). This new approach to teaching and curriculum implementation in physical education is behavior modification. The research findings and techniques from behavior modification are now just beginning to be introduced into physical education. As will be seen in the following pages, the behavior modification approach in physical education has already been demonstrated to be very effective. It is clear that the behavior modification approach promises to be used very extensively in the gymnasium in the future, just as it is presently being so widely and successfully used in many other areas of education. Because of the initial and continuing success of applying behavior modification principles and teaching procedures to physical education settings, behavioral procedures potentially offer a great deal of promise in helping teachers to translate their physical education curricula into practice.

Physical Education's Concern with Behavior Modification

A look at physical education publications vividly shows that the behavior modification approach has not yet received the kind of attention many other areas of education have given it. Up until now the behavior modification approach has been severely neglected in physical education literature, and by physical education teachers themselves. (149) One example of this neglect was noted in 1972 when it was mentioned that the most recent 10-year index of the *Research Quarterly* did not list "reinforcement" as a topic. (208) But as early as 1967 a suggestion was made to use behavior modification in teaching swimming (185), and a few years later perhaps one of the first applications of behavior modification in a physical education setting appeared. It demonstrated that dispensing candy or pennies was more effective in getting individuals to swim more laps than a standard coaching procedure. (188)

The problem of applying behavior modification to a technology of physical education has been seen as that of finding ways to utilize the general principles of behavior in specific physical education settings. (186) One early, ingenious study provided constant feedback to a swimmer by using a pen light. The beam of light was focused into the eye of the swimmer as he was swimming the butterfly stroke, signaling his correct and incorrect responses. This study was very successful in translating the behavioral principles of feedback into a practical procedure for the swimming coach to use for teaching. (186,187) In 1972 two important publications appeared, but they have not had the positive influence on physical education practice they perhaps should have had. Most probably physical educators at that time were unfamiliar with behavior modification, and both publications were too technical for those with very limited backgrounds in this approach. One publication, appearing in the *Research Quarterly,* was a somewhat formidable theoretical article proposing how a behavioral approach might be useful in physical education and consisted of a long list of definitions of behavioral principles. (208) The other publication was a very comprehensive and detailed (but not very practical) book. (189) Both of these publications argued that behavioral procedures could, and should, be extensively studied and used in physical education settings for the two basic purposes of developing sport skills and maintaining them over time.

Other suggestions for using behavioral procedures based on behavior modification (60) or "reality therapy" (117) have recently appeared, as well as some very cursory descriptions of contracts (63) or tokens (147) in physical education. While for some time now physical educators have focused some of their attention on the use of behavior modification in physical education, the amount of work completed hasn't been very extensive. But regardless of the limited practical work done up to now, many of the suggestions and arguments which have been made for incorporating the behavior modification approach into physical education make very good sense. This is especially true in terms of the current concerns to make physical education research more relevant and teaching more objective and accountable. Although the experimental work in behavior modification within physical education is itself limited, its future is very encouraging. But much work remains.

In view of the initial attempts of physical educators to utilize behavior modification, it should be of interest to them that others too have been actively working with behavior modification procedures as techniques to improve physical fitness and athletic skills. This work has been going on now for some years and has been very successful, for it has had extensive applications that are direct and immediate to physical education practice. This work is being done by individuals trained in behavioral procedures who have been directly applying the behavior modification approach to the study and improvement of motor behaviors, physical fitness, and athletic skills. When one takes into account the combined interest and present experimental findings of researchers both within and without physical education, one is forced to conclude that application of the behavior modification approach to physical education is more than merely promising.

Behavior Modification's Concern with Physical Education

Behavior modification practictioners have performed a wide variety of studies which bear directly on physical education practice. In addition to dealing with the development of various motor skills and athletic behaviors, their studies have also dealt with such common kinds of teaching problems as classroom control, completing assignments, attendance, etc. (178,230) Several very important points should be kept in mind when considering the possibilities of applying the behavior modification approach to physical education settings. First, one should be aware of the fact that the behavior modification approach is not laboratory experimentation. It is applied research which is done in the real world, with real people and real problems. Thus the findings mentioned in this report were obtained from teachers or others working and interacting in their everyday natural settings. There is no extrapolation from the laboratory, from mental tests of various kinds, or other kinds of testing, to real-life settings. The behavior modification approach deals directly with the concerns of the physical education teacher, and because of this the research is directly applicable to the classroom or gymnasium.

The behavior modification approach, being an applied experimental approach, allows teachers to conduct their own experiments in their own settings. It allows them to measure the behaviors they want to improve before they try to improve upon them, to manipulate their teaching procedures systematically in some manner, and to evaluate continually the effects of their procedures, all while they are teaching. The behavior modification approach in physical education thus fits into the mainstream of current thought for making physical education research and practice more relevant, accountable, and effective.

The second important point to keep in mind (the first being that the behavior modification approach is not laboratory experimentation) is that the behavior modification approach in physical education is very general in its applications. Thus the same behavioral principles and procedures would be used by the physical education teacher for improving any physical fitness or sports-related skills, regardless of the kinds of individuals being taught, or their ages. That is, the same behavioral principles and procedures would be used if one were concerned with improving the accuracy of the tennis serve, the number of sit-ups done in one minute, the percentage of successfully completed basketball free-throw shots, the completion of class-written assignments, the number of times a student talks back to the teacher, or the number of individuals in a group who come to class late or run around wildly. Similarly, the same behavioral principles and procedures would be used with young nursery school children, elementary, middle school, high school, or college-aged students, middle-aged adults, or even geriatric patients. The same is true if any of them are categorized as normal, retarded, autistic, schizophrenic, brain damaged, emotionally disturbed, etc.

When physical education teachers use the behavior modification approach in their classes, they use many of the same behavioral principles and procedures—regardless of what behavior and whose. But, depending upon the specific situation, the procedures one uses to implement particular behavioral principles can be varied to accommodate the particular characteristics of the individuals involved, or whatever other restrictions present. That is, the behavioral principles being used would always remain the same, e.g., reinforcement and shaping, but the particular way of implementing them as teaching procedures can vary slightly from situation to situation.

As behavioral studies demonstrate, it is very fortunate that the same behavioral principles can be applied to different situations with minor variations in the procedures. This makes the behavior modification approach much easier for all involved. Consider how fortunate we are to have such a happy state of affairs. Physical education teachers, like most teachers, are especially concerned about discipline problems and controlling their classes. (184,207) So it should be somewhat reassuring to realize that the very same behavioral principles and procedures a physical education teacher would use to teach good posture could also be used with minor variations to improve the performance of a whole class of students cleaning up after gym. A common concern of secondary level teachers (184)—as well as for physical education teachers at all levels—is setting up adaptive physical education programs for students with physical or other disabilities. Because behavioral procedures are applicable to any kind of individual, physical education teachers, and especially those actively involved in adaptive physical education (46), should welcome the fact that similar teaching procedures can be used both with regular students and with students who need adaptive physical education experiences. Once physical educators learn the relevant behavioral principles and become familiar with the technicalities of the behavioral approach and somewhat proficient in its use, then they can apply the approach to all of their students, regardless of their ages, disabilities, or classroom situations.

The reason why the behavior modification approach has such a wide and seemingly unlimited applicability is, very simply, because the approach is an applied experimental technique. The experimental approach, because of its very nature, has unlimited possibilities for assisting anyone in the teaching of physical education behaviors, or any other kinds of behaviors. (7,44) To appreciate the extensive applications which behavior modification procedures can have in physical education, consider now some of the ways behavior modification practitioners have been successfully using this approach in improving physical fitness, motor, and athletic skills.

Walking behavior has been successfully induced in a number of behavior modification studies. Several of these studies dealt with individuals who constantly crawled although they could walk. In one of these studies merely praising a nursery schoolchild when she was walking and ignoring her when she was crawling resulted in her walking instead of crawling. (83) Another study with nursery schoolchildren who were profoundly mentally retarded used a combination of several behavioral procedures to get them to stop crawling and walk instead. (161) They were praised when they walked, and restrained momentarily when they crawled. Behavioral procedures have also been used to teach a mentally retarded *spina bifida* child to use crutches. (89) They have been also used in various ways to teach a number of other mentally retarded individuals to walk. (111,150,197) Part of the actual training of one of these studies (150) can be seen in a portion of the movie *Rewards and Reinforcement* which can be easily obtained for rental through any audiovisual center. Geriatric patients in their 80's and 90's have also been taught to walk with behavioral procedures instead of using their wheelchairs. (129,190)

The behavior modification approach has also been used to improve the poor posture of individuals. In one study a 13-year-old emotionally disturbed boy's praying-mantis-like posture was improved by using a combination of direct postural training, which had him match silhouettes of his own good and poor posture, and token training, where tokens were given for exhibiting good posture. (57) In other studies the posture of a number of normal adults was improved by having them wear a mechanical apparatus which automatically provided them with feedback throughout the day whenever they were slouching. Either a tone would come on, or they would receive vibrotactile stimulation from the devices when they slouched. Both procedures were very effective in improving the posture of these adults. (6,160)

Children's playing, climbing, and use of various kinds of outdoor equipment has also been studied. By simply, but systematically, praising young nursery school children for approaching and climbing monkey bars the frequency with which they did so increased substantially in several studies done with normal children. (30,97) Another study found that verbally praising a young child for climbing a monkey bar was very effective in getting him to do so more often, even though the child was severely brain damaged. (79) Systematic behavioral procedures combined with a consumable reinforcement of sweetened cereal have been used to teach a young retarded child to ride a tricycle (171), while the use of a token system has been quite successful in getting other retarded children to increase the percentage of time they spent on competitive play situations in which only one of them would be a winner. (110)

The behavioral improvement of athletic skills and sports behaviors has been demonstrated in a number of different settings. In a study of swimming, mentally retarded adolescents substantially improved their backstroke and sidestroke when given task-specific verbal praise and corrections for their performance. (70) In another swimming study, behavioral procedures were applied to an entire competitive swimming team of 32 boys and girls ranging in age from 9 to 16. (149) The rationale for this study was based on the idea that an athlete's self-recording of his or her own performance may function to provide sufficient feedback to reinforce his or her behavior. In the study mentioned earlier as perhaps the first application of behavior modification in physical education, candy and money were found to be effective in increasing the number of laps swum. (188) The experimenters also had simultaneously recorded the number of laps each swimmer swam on a public program board and mentioned that they suspected that the program boards alone may have affected the number of laps swum: they singled it out as a possible variable to study more extensively in the future.

To test their hypothesis one of the original experimenters in this early study experimentally manipulated the self-recording of behaviors and the use of program boards with the swim team in order to try to improve two different behaviors, attendance at practice, and the number of laps swum during practice. Each team member recorded his attendance on a public attendance board and the number of laps swum on a public program board. This self-recording not only decreased absences, but when applied to several other related inappropriate behaviors, being tardy or leaving early, it also decreased them. The number of 25-yard laps completed for the swimmers whose data were reported in the study showed that these swimmers increased the number of laps they swam by 27.1 percent when they were self-recording their own performance on the program boards. This represented approximately 619 additional yards that each of these swimmers swam compared to their normal workouts without the program boards. The important aspect of this study that deserves note is that the swimmers were actively involved in providing their own feedback for their performance and providing themselves with self-direction. The public program board made, not only themselves, but others around them very much aware of their performance. This objective and public awareness of one's performance is a very important component of all behavioral studies done in physical education, or other settings. It should be mentioned that during the course of this study this regional swimming team went from the obscurity of sixth place to the prominance of placing second in the province of Nova Scotia, Canada.

A similar type of feedback program combined with a token system has been very successfully used to improve the pole vaulting of two 15-year-old high school students. (21) Before the study began neither of them had jumped nine feet for almost a whole year. But after less than 15 workouts using the behavioral approach of receiving tokens for increasing their pole vaulting, and having their performances publicly recorded on a chart (a lined figure) which was posted on the bulletin board of the locker room, one of them was jumping at 10 feet, and the other at 10 feet, 6 inches. Their tokens could be exchanged for a milkshake or for the privilege of missing a workout. Both of them preferred missing workouts, a high status activity. So without any cost to the coach, and with the athletes even missing practice, but contingent upon their doing well in previous practices, the performance of these two students was very substantially improved.

The behavioral approach has also been used to improve the rule-following and clean-up behaviors of students. One study in a college weight-lifting room dealt with the problem of decreasing the number of barbells, dumbbells, and weight plates left on tne floor each day. (49) It was a problem in neatness, but more importantly it was also a serious problem in safety. A variety of procedures were systematically applied to improve this situation. The first procedure, posting signs with the rules of the weight room, reduced the number of articles on the floor somewhat. Next, signs coupled with tokens in the form of points for putting things away was tried. The individual with the greatest number of points could turn them in for a variety of things (record albums, movie passes, or dinner at a restaurant). This combined procedure was more effective than the signs alone. The most effective procedure that was tried was a group behavior modification technique. In this procedure closing the weight-lifting room was threatened if the number of items on the floor exceeded a certain number. This procedure was the most effective of them all, and additionally illustrates, as did the study with the swim team (149), that the behavioral approach can be just as easily applied to a whole group of individuals, as to a single person.

A similar kind of group behavior modification procedure has been used to improve the rule-following of the between 11 and 72 children who used an urban recreation center each evening. (173) A group contingency was used for the whole group present any evening in which minutes of their recreation time would be lost for various rule infractions, e.g., a loss of one minute for each coat not hung up, or pool rack not hung, and 15 minutes loss for damage to cues or cue tips, broken Ping-Pong balls or paddles, or arguments. Any time a fight occurrred everyone had to leave immediately for the night. The rule violations were greatly reduced when this group behavior modification procedure was systematically used in the recreation center.

This same study also used recreation time as a reinforcement for individuals who brought new members to the recreation center. When regular membership drives were held, on the average less than one new member per day was recruited. But this jumped to five new members per day when a member received recreation time as a reinforcing consequence for bringing a new member to the center. When this reinforcement procedure was being used, each member bringing in a new member could come to the recreation center an hour before opening time and could engage in any activity of their choice. This allowed them to play their favorite games without having to wait in line or having others around disturbing them.

Getting individuals to exercise daily can be quite difficult. Behavioral procedures have been used to increase exercising in geriatric patients (123) by giving them tokens for each three revolutions they made on a stationary bicycle. Each three revolutions resulted in a token automatically being delivered through a slot that they could turn in for extra cigarettes, chewing gum, or peanuts. This procedure was very effective in increasing their exercising. Keeping physically fit and exercising daily is of increasing concern to many. Teaching individuals how to do this on their own is an important concern of physical educators and also those working in behavior modification. What this involves is teaching individuals self-control procedures so that they can effectively manage their own physical fitness. (246:85–105)

Long-term, self-motivated exercising of individuals is one of the most important goals of physical education, and the behavioral approach can be used to help people accomplish this. Examples of how adults can use behavioral self-control procedures to meet their exercise goals will be discussed in some detail in a later section of this report.

What Behavior Modification Offers Physical Education—Now!

If one compares the preceeding summary of applications of the behavior modification approach with traditional physical education approaches and current trends, it is apparent that the behavioral approach fits in very nicely with contemporary concerns for objectivity, accountability, relevance, and effectiveness in both physical education research and teaching. The direct applicability and relevance of the behavior modification approach makes it very reasonable to conclude that it has much to offer physical education—now! In general this approach offers physical education an applied and experimentally oriented methodology for effectively transforming physical education curricula into practice. (7,17) Specifically the behavior modification approach offers physical education:

1. Extensive research findings of various kinds directly applicable to the work of the physical education teacher in the gym.
2. A set of behavioral principles and applied experimental procedures which can be used to help implement and evaluate physical education curricula, and improve many motor, athletic, health, and social behaviors of daily concern to the physical education teacher. These principles and procedures can be used by any school personnel, by paraprofessionals, and by students themselves and their parents.
3. Relevant, objective, accountable, effective, and positive teaching, evaluation, and record-keeping procedures which will facilitate the active, successful cooperation and communication among all members of the educational community, including parents, so

that they can work together to improve the physical fitness and athletic skills of the students.

In order to help physical educators use behavior modification as an adjunct for implementing their curricula, the remainder of this report will discuss the technicalities of the behavioral approach. Although not exhaustive or inclusive, the information in this report should be sufficiently detailed to enable one to apply a number of behavioral procedures in a variety of ways to one's own setting. However, it must be remembered that this report is but a detailed introduction to the applications of the behavior modification approach to physical education. By using the information in it as basic source material, and by reading and mastering its more important references, the reader should become proficient in the fundamentals of this approach. Becoming proficient involves three distinct and equally important processes: acquiring a sufficient knowledge of the basic principles of behavior, learning how these behavioral principles are implemented as various behavioral improvement procedures, and becoming conversant with the results of behavioral research studies directly relevant to physical education.

How successful physical educators will be depends upon the extent to which they master these three interrelated aspects of the behavioral approach, in addition to the extent to which they gain practical experience in using this approach with their students. But the job doesn't stop there. Because the behavioral approach is experimentally and data oriented, new experimental results and data are appearing in each new issue of the many different professional journals, and specific behavioral improvement procedures are being constantly researched and improved upon. As a result of this, individuals involved in this approach are constantly keeping up with their study of behavioral research as it becomes available in the literature, and they are constantly refining their actual applications of behavioral procedures as suggested in the latest articles. Those physical educators who decide to incorporate aspects of the behavior modification approach into their own work will also have to do this. If they succeed, then the results of their efforts should be reflected positively in the improved motor, athletic, and health behaviors of their students.

BEHAVIOR MODIFICATION = BEHAVIOR IMPROVEMENT

Because the behavior modification approach is so new, the public, many in the helping professions, and teachers of all kinds are unaware of exactly what it is, what it has done, and what it has to offer. Few practicing physical education teachers have had the opportunity to be exposed to behavior modification during their college courses, and fewer yet have had a whole course in behavior modification. Thus it is inevitable that many misconceptions and criticisms have been expressed. (154,155,249) These criticisms are primarily due to an ignorance of the behavior modification approach. Rejoinders to such misconceptions and criticisms are readily available. (162,165) Those who are knowledgeable about the details of this approach consider it to be very positive (38), and for the following reasons (158):

1. It extends success and reinforcements to many who may never have experienced success or reinforcement, or only a minimal amount.
2. It emphasizes removing punitive-type procedures from educational practices, substituting positive ones.
3. It helps teachers to systematize what they have been doing correctly for many years so that they can teach more effectively in the future.
4. It is objective and accountable and demands better teaching, because it makes teachers systematically observe and analyze what they are doing and what effects their teaching procedures have on their students.

The behavior modification approach is really nothing but using experimentally demonstrated, effective, and positive teaching procedures. The name "behavior modification" may make individuals think of controlling, manipulating, and forcing students to change their behaviors, but this is not the case. It's impossible to change the name and the meaning which has been associated with it overnight, but a better, and more descriptive term for the behavior modification approach is *behavior improvement*. The behavior modification approach in physical education, then, is concerned with improving those physical fitness, athletic, motor, or social behaviors in the gym class which are prescribed by the curriculum or by the professional judgment of the physical education teacher. Although some individuals engaged in using this approach may refer to themselves as "behavior modifiers," or be called that by others, all of them would agree that the best synonym for this very, very formidable term would simply be "teacher." Regardless of who is using the behavior modification approach they are all teachers, trying to teach and guide others in improving their behaviors. They are really "behavior improvers."

As was mentioned before, in order to comprehend and use the behavior modification approach, one must have a thorough understanding of behavioral principles, of practical techniques for using these behavioral principles as behavior improvement procedures, and of the experimental methodology on which all this is based. These aspects of the behavior modification approach are discussed on the following pages.

Operant Conditioning

Technically, behavior modification is the application of operant conditioning principles to changing and improving behaviors. Operant conditioning is a very well established area of learning research which is primarily concerned with how consequences, or events that follow behaviors, affect the frequency of occurrence of the behaviors in the future. When one objectively observes and experimentally studies the behaviors of individuals in real-life settings in the home, institution, and the school, it becomes self-evident that what happens following a behavior is very important.

Why did the gym teacher send you back to your homeroom, Susan?

Because I called the gym teacher a "stupid idiot!"

Why did you do that?

I always call the gym teacher a "stupid idiot" when he makes things too hard, and I want to come back to my homeroom.

Although the laboratory research in this area has been very extensive for many years, the systematic study of how consequences affect what children and adults do in everyday life and the gymnasium is, of course, relatively new. It is difficult for most people to stand back and look at what is happening to them in an objective, scientific, and dispassionate manner, but this is exactly what the experimental methodology of the behavior modification approach permits us to do. When one masters the details of this approach, and applies it appropriately, it allows us to see objectively what we and others are doing. This new way of looking at what is happening in our everyday lives is oftentimes very revealing. Consider the cartoon about Susan and her gym teacher.

Why did Susan call her gym teacher a "stupid idiot"? Although typical interpretations might revolve around "home problems," "aggressiveness," "immaturities," being "unmotivated," or whatever, Susan did it for a consequence—being sent back to her classroom. Unintentionally the teacher was reinforcing Susan for calling him a stupid idiot, because whenever Susan did that the gym teacher sent her back to her homeroom. Just as Susan's gym teacher has learned that coming to work every day will result in the consequence of a pay check every now and then, Susan has learned that calling her gym teacher a name will result in the consequence of being sent back to her homeroom.

Antecedents of Behaviors

Although the work in operant conditioning is concerned primarily with how consequences affect behaviors, it is also concerned with how antecedents (events which precede behaviors) affect the occurrence of a behavior or its termination. For most behaviors one can rather easily find some observable event or antecedent which, in essence, controls the behaviors. When you come to a green light you keep on driving, but when you come to a red light you stop. When your clock at home says 7:30 a.m., or so, you start to go to work, and when a clock at school says 3:00 p.m., or so, you stop working. Many events caused by inanimate objects precede our behaviors, starting or stopping them in various ways. A big sign on a furniture store that says "75% Off Everything in the Store" should get many a passerby to start walking to the door. But if a small sign on the door says "Closed Today," they will stop and walk away.

Not only can events such as these function as antecedents, but more importantly, "animate" events, events of various kinds coming from other people, also function as antecedents to start and stop behaviors. A gym teacher may say, "Stand in a straight line," which may start a behavior, or, "Be quiet!" which may stop a behavior. Being aware of both the antecedents and the consequences of behaviors is very important because a particular antecedent may get a behavior started, and some particular consequence may keep it going or increase it in the future. Look at the cartoon again. When Susan's homeroom teacher asked her why she sassed her gym teacher, Susan said, "I always call the gym teacher a 'stupid idiot' when he makes things too hard and I want to come back to my homeroom." The antecedent to Susan's sassing was her gym teacher's making things too hard. Susan's sassing may have begun when her teacher gave her a particularly difficult thing to do in the gym one day, something beyond her ability at the time. Susan may have spontaneously said that the gym teacher was a "stupid idiot," not particularly in any malicious way, but, for whatever reason, the teacher followed this remark with a consequence for Susan. He sent her back to her homeroom. Assuming that Susan's homeroom was a more pleasant place to be that day than in the gym trying things which were much too difficult for her, she may have learned almost immediately that the way to escape the gym teacher's class

TABLE 1—THE ABC'S OF THE
BEHAVIOR MODIFICATION APPROACH

A	B	C
Antecedent	*Behavior*	*Consequence*
difficult task	"Stupid teacher!"	sent to homeroom
heavy weights	attempt to lift, fail	criticized
light weights	attempt to lift, lift	praised
"You're going to be trouble today?"	"Yeah, you dumbbell!"	sent to principal
"Stand in line!"	stand in line	nothing
unknown (???)	crying	talk to child

was to sass the teacher. All of this may go on quite unintentionally and may first happen quite accidentally. Additionally the individuals involved in such a situation may not be able to verbalize exactly what is going on as well as Susan. Because people are actively involved in these situations they usually can't see what is happening. But once they realize that their behaviors, and those of others, are dependent upon antecedents and consequences in their environments, then they can begin to unravel the mystery of how anyone's behaviors become established, maintained, or discarded.

The behavior modification approach is concerned with how behaviors are learned and how they persist. Both antecedents and consequences are important to understand if one wants to improve behaviors in the gym or on the playing field. The behavioral approach is concerned with three main events: the antecedents of behaviors, the behaviors themselves, and the consequences which follow these behaviors. What this all boils down to are the ABC's, as you can see in the Table 1.

In Susan's case, the difficult task her gym teacher gave her was the antecedent (or cue, or stimulus) for her to call her teacher a name. After the name-calling she received the consequence of being sent back to her homeroom. The antecedents which precede behaviors not only affect whether a behavior will occur or not, but they also can affect whether a behavior is performed successfully or not, and in addition they can also affect the kinds of consequences which will follow the behavior. If a gym teacher gives a student weights which are too heavy, this antecedent will result in failure, and the teacher might follow this with the consequence of criticism, even though the failure wasn't the student's fault. But if the teacher gave lighter weights, the student most probably would have lifted them, and the teacher probably would have followed the student's performance with praise, as a consequence.

If a teacher makes a critical remark to a student before he or she begins to do anything, like, "You're going to be trouble today?", this antecedent might cause the student to talk back to the teacher: "Yeah, you dumbbell!" This can be followed by the consequence of being sent to the principal's office. In school settings curricular materials of various kinds, physical events, and—very importantly— the social events coming from the teacher and other students can function as important antecedents which can start or stop behaviors in various ways. Just as Susan's gym teacher accidentally produced the problem he had with Susan by giving her too difficult a task to perform, so teachers can produce similar kinds of problems by how they talk to their students. They may accidentally make their statements antecedents that start or stop behaviors.

Even though an antecedent provided by a teacher, such as "Stand in line!", may actually produce the behavior the teacher wants, a teacher may forget the other half of his or her job, which is providing consequences. So in some instances a teacher may consistently tell students to stand in line, but may never say anything nice when they do so. In the future they may not stand in line quite so fast, or not as often, or not as well as they initially did, and the teacher may begin to wonder why. Keeping the ABC's constantly in mind will help anyone from making this mistake. In a number of instances it may be difficult or impossible to see what the antecedent of a behavior may be. For example a student may suddenly begin to cry in class, but no observable antecedent may be apparent. Regardless of this, a consequence may occur every time the child cries. The teacher may talk to the child each time crying occurs, and this may accidentally increase the crying. When one cannot isolate any possible antecedents, consequences can always be changed.

Whenever a particular behavior is judged important enough by a teacher to be improved, one should first watch what is going on for several days in order to get a good picture of exactly what is happening. One should ask the following two questions, and keep a record of what is happening:

1. What happened *just before* the behavior occurred? What did I do or say, or what did someone else do or say? What curricular materials were being used, or what training procedures were being used? What were the possible antecedents for the behavior?

2. What happened *just after* the behavior? What did I do or what did someone else do or say? (Maybe nothing happened.) What kind of consequences followed the behavior?

By focusing in on these two things which surround every behavior, one can quickly begin to see possible factors which may be affecting the behavior in various ways. Isolating possible antecedents will help one to see what is getting a behavior going, or what might be stopping it. Isolating consequences will help one to see what might be maintaining the behavior, or what might be increasing the frequency of the behavior. By systematically changing either or both of these events, one should be able to improve the behavior.

Using Consequences to Improve Behaviors in the Gymnasium

Because we aren't used to, or more correctly, haven't been taught to watch objectively what is going on as we interact with others, it's difficult to be aware of the consequences of our behaviors or the extent to which they are affecting our own behaviors and those of the individuals we interact with. Turn on a TV, a light, or the engine in your car, and you get consequences for your behaviors. Make the appropriate kinds of motor responses with a pen, pencil, piece of chalk, or the keys of a typewriter, and you will also produce consequences for your behaviors. Life is full of these kinds of "inanimate" consequences which are happening to everyone hundreds and hundreds of times each day. But the most important kinds of consequences each of us gets each day comes from other people, husbands and wives, sons and daughters, parents, supervisors, foremen, and managers in work settings, and in schools, teachers, students, principals, and other members of the school staff.

The vast amount of work which has been done using the behavior modification approach in schools has demonstrated that teachers are the most important source of consequences for their students' academic and social behaviors. Not only are teachers important in this respect, but as previously noted, they are also very important in providing students with antecedents. So whatever a teacher does, either before or after a student behaves, can influence the student's behavior in some fashion for better or for worse. Now consider the nature of two very important types of consequences teachers provide their students, reinforcement and punishment. Although everyone freely uses these terms, many times they use them incorrectly. Both reinforcement and punishment have very technical meanings.

REINFORCEMENT

The technical definition of reinforcement as it is used by laboratory workers in operant conditioning research and as it is used by practitioners of the behavior modification approach is *any event following a behavior which increases the occurrence of the behavior in the future.* That Susan was sent back to her homeroom after sassing her teacher had the effect of increasing her sassing, and thus it was reinforcement. Think of the last time you hugged someone. What happened afterward? Did this person hug you in return? Could it have been a reinforcement for you? What do you think would happen to your hugging if no one hugged you in return? What do you think would happen to your teaching if you were never paid again? There is no doubt that consequences are important for increasing and maintaining the frequencies of our behaviors.

The most important kind of reinforcing consequences students get in school, behavioral research shows, comes from their teachers. (80,107,130,133) These consequences which teachers give to their students consist of various aspects of the teachers' own social behaviors. They include praises, criticisms, pats on the head, nods, frowns, smiles, and other forms of attention. Although educational researchers have been descriptively recording and categorizing a wide variety of teacher behaviors, such as "reflecting" and "criticizing" (159,198), and dispensing "comparative," "explicative," "prescriptive," and other kinds of feedback (66), they haven't been looking upon these various teacher behaviors as im-

TABLE 2–SOME EXAMPLES OF CONSEQUENCES WHICH MAY FUNCTION AS REINFORCEMENTS

Behavior	Consequence	Effect on Behavior	What is it?
sassing gym teacher	sent back to homeroom	increases sassing	reinforcement
running 15 feet	marble	increases speed of running	reinforcement
walking	praise	increases walking	reinforcement
pole vaulting	tokens	increases height jumped	reinforcement
standing up	"Sit down!"	increases standing	reinforcement
swimming laps of pool	self-recording of laps swum	increases laps swum	reinforcement

portant consequences for students. Behavioral researchers, in contrast to educational researchers, who have primarily conducted descriptive kinds of research, have tried to analyze experimentally the effects of a teacher's behavior on students. They have found that students' behaviors change systematically when teachers experimentally modulate the social consequences they give to their students. Other kinds of consequences given by teachers can also have the effect of increasing students' behaviors, and thus they too are technically reinforcements. Among these kinds of consequences are giving students free time, prizes, material objects of various kinds, and special kinds of privileges. Consider the examples in Table 2 of some of the kinds of consequences teachers can provide students.

Suppose Susan's teacher sent her back to her homeroom every time she sassed as a punishment for sassing. Since Susan's sassing actually increased in frequency, sending her back to her homeroom was a reinforcement. This gym teacher would have been accidentally, and unknowingly, producing his own problem. Many other consequences can function as reinforcements, as Table 2 illustrates. Young children will run faster down a 15-foot runway if they get a marble than if they don't get one. (201) As previously mentioned, young children (83), retarded individuals (111,150), and geriatric patients (129,190) will walk if they are praised for doing so. Getting tokens for increasing the height of one's pole vaults has been shown to increase pole vaulting performance (21), and self-recording of the laps swum has been shown to increase the number of laps swum. (149) In each of these published studies a variety of different kinds of consequences was used. Regardless of its nature, each consequence had the effect of increasing the frequency of the behavior it followed; in effect, each functioned as a reinforcement.

A number of published studies have shown that a teacher's best intentions can backfire. The kind of problem that Susan's gym teacher had does occur in real life situations. In one study, teachers who had a lot of students standing up in class systematically increased their sit-down commands. They caught more and more children standing up, and again and again told them to sit down. They thought that increasing commands would reduce the number of students standing. But what actually happened was that more students stood up. This procedure was repeated several times. When the teachers increased their sit-down commands more students stood up, and when they decreased their sit-down commands fewer students stood up. The study clearly demonstrated that the increased sit-down commands were functioning as reinforcements for standing up. (131) Criticizing children or adults for inappropriate behaviors can reinforce these undesirable behaviors.

A reinforcement, by definition, must work in order to be labeled as such. The consequence following a behavior must increase the frequency of the behavior before it can be called a reinforcement. A teacher may say, "I praise my swimmers all the time, I'm always reinforcing them." But if their swimming doesn't improve, then the gym teacher isn't describing the situation correctly. The swimmers may be given praise, but if the praise doesn't improve their swimming it doesn't serve as a reinforcement for the swimmers. Just labeling something a reinforcement, or a punishment, for that matter, isn't enough. What counts is whether the behavior followed by this consequence occurs again or improves. When a coach says, "I reinforce my players by giving them decals on their helmets, but they don't get any better," the coach isn't describing what's happening accurately. True, this coach is giving the players decals as consequences for their behaviors, but since their behaviors don't improve, the decals are just consequences, not reinforcements. Prizes are generally considered to be rewards, as is receiving money for doing something. But these consequences should only be called reinforcements after it has been determined that they have had the effect of increasing or improving some behavior in some fashion.

Regardless of the nature of the consequence which follows a behavior, if the behavior increases in frequency, that consequence is functioning as a reinforcement. Therefore criticizing a student, sending a student out of the gym, or letting a student practice can be reinforcements, if they improve or increase the frequency of the behavior they follow. If a behavior does not increase in frequency or improve following a consequence, then that consequence isn't a reinforcement, even though the event, giving someone a plaque, putting his or her name in the newspaper, praising him or her in front of classmates, or whatever, is considered to be a reward by a teacher, a parent, or anyone else. To determine why an event generally recognized as a reward doesn't function as a reinforcement is another problem. The fact remains that the only way to determine if a consequence is a reinforcement or not is by observing its effects in the future on the behavior it followed. Regardless of the nature of the consequence, if it increases a behavior it is a reinforcement—even a punishment such as spanking. A knowledge of this single fact alone takes a great deal of mystery out of many common achievements and failures physical educators have in the gymnasium and on the playing field.

PUNISHMENT

Punishment is technically defined as *any event following a behavior which decreases the occurrence of that behavior in the future.* Just like the definition of reinforcement, the definition of punishment is defined in terms of the effects a particular consequence has on a behavior in the future. The definition of punishment does not depend upon what the consequence is nor upon what a teacher thinks should be a punishment, but rather whether or not it decreases the frequency of the behavior it follows. If Susan's gym teacher said, "I punish Susan every time she sasses me by sending her back to her homeroom," he may have thought that he was punishing Susan.

But was he really? He was actually reinforcing Susan's sassing because that consequence actually increased her sassing. So there may be a difference between what one says one is doing (or what one would like to have happen), and what is actually happening. The only way teachers can know what is happening is by watching objectively what happens when they follow certain behaviors with various kinds of consequences. If a consequence that immediately and consistently follows a behavior a number of times doesn't result in a decrease in the frequency of that behavior, then that consequence is not a punishment—regardless of what it is or what a teacher or anyone else may say about it.

It isn't uncommon for physical education teachers to have a number of set kinds of punishment that they may use in their attempts to decrease the frequency of behaviors they consider to be inappropriate in their students. Students may be sent back to their homerooms or to the principal's office, or they may be made to practice more by doing more exercises or swimming more laps. In each case the intent of the teacher is to decrease the frequency of an inappropriate behavior. Whether or not this actually happens, though, is unpredictable.

In an article concerned with motivating football players, one suggestion for motivating players was to give them a scolding in order to anger them. It was hoped that the anger produced by the scolding would help push a player on to greater success, and that it would also decrease various kinds of errors the player may have been making. (218:73) This suggestion is but one example of the kinds of anecdotal advice found in physical education publications which may sound good and seem to make sense. The suggestion, however, isn't stated specifically enough to be of any practical use to the physical education teacher or coach. The most important problem with such suggestions is that they don't indicate what behavioral principle is being used to obtain the desired results. This is why they are merely bags of tricks. When one looks at the scolding suggestion objectively, it is clear that the scolding is meant to function as a punishment procedure. The football player is scolded following each error so as to decrease his errors. In order to see if the scolding actually functions as a punishment, one would have to keep a record of the various kinds of errors a player makes before even trying out this motivational procedure. Once the record of er-

TABLE 3–SOME EXAMPLES OF CONSEQUENCES WHICH MAY FUNCTION AS PUNISHMENTS

Behavior	Consequence	Effect on Behavior	What is it?
talking out	self-recording of talking	decreased talk-outs	punishment
hitting	sitting in chair	decreased hitting	punishment
getting out of seat on school bus	turning off music	decreased out-of-seats	punishment
breaking recreation rules	loss of recreation time	decreased rule breaking	punishment
leaving weights	close weight room	decreased weights on floor	punishment

rors is obtained, then one can try out the scolding procedure systematically by immediately and consistently following each error with a scolding. At the same time one would have to again keep a record of the player's errors. If the second record contains fewer errors than the first, then the scolding functioned as a punishment. If the second record contains more errors than the first record, then the scolding functioned as a reinforcement.

The two concepts, reinforcement and punishment, are defined in terms of the effects they have on a behavior in the future. Any consequence may function as a punishment if it consistently follows a behavior and decreases the frequency of that behavior. Knowing the definition of punishment can be very helpful to teachers. Table 3 gives some examples of consequences which may function as punishments.

Having students record their own behaviors after they occur can change them in various ways. A student's talking-out may decrease if the student records each instance of it immediately. (23) If so, self-recording would be functioning as a punishment, and the student would, in effect, be punishing him or herself. Earlier we saw that self-recording can function as a reinforcement (149): the number of laps swum increased after the swimmers began recording the number of laps they swam. Thus simply recording one's own behavior can function as either a reinforcement or a punishment. Having a child sit in a chair for two minutes immediately after the child hits someone may decrease the child's hitting (237) and thus function as a punishment. This procedure is exactly like one used in hockey where a player is sent to the penalty box after sticking an opponent. This kind of punishment procedure, called time-out, has been extensively studied. (14)

Punishment procedures, just as reinforcement procedures, can be used with an entire group of individuals. (86) A group time-out procedure has been used with a bus full of students to reduce their out-of-seat behaviors—a dangerous behavior on a moving school bus. Rock-and-roll music was played during the bus rides, but was immediately turned off if any of the children got out of their seats. This group time-out procedure was very effective. (183) This particular procedure, as well as others (29), offers an effective way for gym teachers and coaches to decrease inappropriate behaviors on buses. Other punishment procedures such as response cost can also be used with entire groups of individuals. Group response cost procedures used in an urban recreation program consisted of depriving the entire group of children of recreation time whenever a rule infraction occurred. Each time an individual broke a rule, a given number of minutes of recreation time was deducted from the time available for the whole group. (173) A similar kind of procedure has been used in a college weight room. The room was closed when the number of weights on the floor exceeded a certain number. This group procedure was also very effective. (49)

Ways to Change and Improve Athletic, Physical Fitness, and Social Behaviors

Physical educators agree that there are numerous important behavioral objectives students should develop in their physical education classes (59,205), at both the elementary (20) and the secondary level. (108) Looking at the physical education of students from the viewpoint of the behavior modification approach, there are basically only three behavioral decisions one can make about any

student's behavior:
1. We are not satisfied with a behavior and want to *increase the behavior* in some way. We may want to increase walking (83), improve posture (160), increase competitive play (110), increase the number of laps swum (149), increase the number of children coming to recreation (173), increase the height of the pole vaults (21), or increase the amount one exercises. (101)
2. We are not satisfied with a behavior and want to *decrease the behavior* in some way. We may want less talking-out (23), less out-of-seat behavior (183), fewer rules broken (173), fewer weights left on the floor (49), or less hitting. (237)
3. We are satisfied with a behavior and decide to *leave it alone*. Being satisfied with the particular aspects of a student's attendance, social interactions with others, exericising, or sports performance, we continue to interact with him or her as usual.

Any attempt to improve a student's behavior in the gymnasium or on the playing field involves either increasing or decreasing behaviors in some fashion. An examination of any guide to physical education (202,235) confirms this conclusion. Guides discuss specific athletic and physical fitness behaviors students should acquire and the various kinds of errors they should try to decrease. In most situations one would usually work simultaneously on decreasing an inappropriate behavior or some sort of an error, and increasing or improving a more appropriate or correct behavior.

The behaviors to be increased in frequency are considered desirable physical fitness, athletic, and social behaviors, and those to be decreased are considered inappropriate physical fitness, athletic, and social behaviors. The inappropriate behaviors to be decreased include social behaviors which produce classroom management or discipline problems. Behavioral studies show that the three most common kinds of social behaviors teachers are interested in decreasing are usually talking-out, out-of-seat, and hitting. The kinds of errors one might want to decrease in physical education settings could include errors of movement, form, execution, etc.

A commonly expressed concern about the behavior modification approach is that the method itself forces teachers to change particular kinds of behaviors or to use particular kinds of procedures. Rest assured that no force or coercion is involved. The decisions about what specific behaviors students should exhibit and thus which behaviors might best be increased or decreased remain the responsibility of the physical education teacher. The behavior modification approach does not specify what behaviors should be improved. It offers a method for effectively implementing such decisions once they are made, and it also offers a variety of tested procedures that a teacher may choose to use for improving these behaviors. Once behavioral goals are established for physical fitness, athletic, and social behaviors, the techniques and procedures of the behavior modification approach can then be used to achieve these curricular or teacher-determined goals. The teacher must decide which behaviors merit improvement, and whether or not to use the behavioral approach. If the behavioral approach is selected one must further select the specific behavioral procedure(s) to use.

METHODOLOGY OF USING BEHAVIOR MODIFICATION PROCEDURES

In applying behavior modification procedures, the teacher is actually engaging in applied research while teaching. (7) Regardless of the setting, age of the student, type of student, or type of behaviors the teacher may want to improve, one follows the same basic set of steps:

1. Pinpoint the behavior (describe it objectively)
2. Record and chart the behavior (count it and keep a visual record)
3. Change the environment (systematically introduce consequences, change antecedents, etc.)
4. Continue to record and chart the behavior in the changed environment
5. Evaluate the change in the environment by the records (has the behavior changed?)
6. Try, try again (re-arrange the environment) if not successful within a week.

The entire sequence must be followed in order for a procedure to qualify as a behavior modification procedure. It isn't uncommon for someone to claim, "I tried behavior modification, but it just doesn't work for me." But was the entire sequence followed? Did the teacher pinpoint the behavior to be changed? Did the teacher keep an objective count and chart of that behavior? Did the teacher systematically manipulate consequences and/or antecedents of that behavior and again record the behavior? Did the teacher compare one record with another? And did the teacher try again if unsuccessful? The chances are that one or more of these basic steps were left out. If not, yet another explanation for the supposed failure of the behavior modification approach lies in the deceptive simplicity of the basic set of steps to be followed. The application of each step requires a firm grasp of specific behavioral information and skills. This information comes from relevant published research and publications of a general nature. There is a great deal of published research dealing with an extensive variety of specific behavioral procedures and with just about any behavior one may want to improve. (121) One must become aware of this body of work, study it, and use it as models for one's own behavior improvement projects. For example, if one were interested in increasing or decreasing the academic or social behaviors of an entire class or team, one could consult a recent publication summarizing group procedures in the schools and offering guidelines for using such procedures. (86) If the behavioral approach doesn't seem to work even though the basic sequence was followed in its entirety, then it is highly likely that no relevant published behavioral studies were consulted for use as models or guides in the behavior improvement project. Thus, failure of the behavioral approach may occur when one does not do the job adequately or well enough.

Even if one has sufficiently pinpointed, recorded, and charted a behavior and has systematically changed the environment by introducing consequences and changing antecedents in some fashion, things may not go well. When this occurs one must examine the procedure analytically. For this reason, it is best to keep records of exactly how one is going about trying to improve behaviors and of the published materials serving as models. Later by looking at this information and by having others look at it to offer their opinions, one may be able to suspect or determine what may have gone wrong. The procedural rules for using consequences as reinforcements or punishments are very important. These rules may not have been followed carefully. The procedures may not be used as they were intended to be used or as they have been used in the past. Or the chosen consequences or antecedents simply don't function as reinforcements or punishments in this particular situation. Once a flaw is suspected or discovered, one can change the procedure and try again. A handy rule of thumb is to use a behavioral approach consistently for around a week. If it is going to work, it should work by then. There is no need to use the same procedure any longer before evaluating, analyzing, and changing it, if necessary. The behavioral approach is not a static approach. The effectiveness of behavioral teaching procedures has to be continuously evaluated as they are being used, and changes in the applications of the procedures must be made as necessary.

The aim of the behavior modification approach is to help individuals learn behaviors which will be of benefit to them. If an evaluation of their progress shows that they are not improving, then the particular teaching procedures being used aren't working. Generally no one, neither student nor teacher, is blamed for the lack of improvement; instead, the lack of improvement is usually attributed to the application of the behavioral principles and procedures in that particular setting. There are many ways in which they can be used incorrectly or inappropriately. The extent to which they are successfully used to help improve students' behaviors is completely dependent upon the extent to which the person using these procedures learns the details of the behavior modification approach.

Pinpointing Behaviors

To use the behavior modification approach in implementing the physical education curriculum, one must begin by dealing with observable behaviors and events. Some particular behavior or some specific aspect of a behavior must be specifically and objectively pinpointed before one can proceed to the next step of this approach. The colloquial expression "What you see, is what you get" could be an apt motto for someone using the behavior modification approach. As long as educators stay at this level of description, problems should be minimal in discussions of how accountable one is in teaching the curriculum.

The nature of many of the goals prescribed by physical education curricula can very easily be made observable and objective. Other curricular prescriptions cannot. One of the outcomes of the increased concern for accountability in physical education (20,64,

108) is an emphasis on specifically defining what students are to do in their gym classes, what behaviors they should be exhibiting. What is needed in physical education, it is argued, are clear-cut behavioral objectives. (205) Although the terms "pinpointing" and "behavioral" or "performance" objectives are not used very often in coaching publications, many articles clearly do use behavioral descriptions of these athletic skills, whether they are talking about teaching hurdle jumping (36), tennis (98), baseball (217), or whatever. So do many books on physical education. (202,235) Even so, a considerable lag in the use of behavioral descriptions is evidenced as one can just as easily find emphases placed on nonbehavioral objectives. Some physical educators argue that it is more important to change "perceptions" (154) than athletic behaviors. A recent curriculum guide gave as some of its objectives, "adaption to stress," "good citizenship," "learning to accept victory and defeat gracefully," and, "knowledge and appreciation" (175), hardly behavioral objectives in the traditional sense. (134) Furthermore, although supposedly discussing "behavioral objectives," many curriculum guides, in fact, may not be very behavioral. (52)

A pinpointed behavior is *a behavior defined so that anyone can see the behavior, count the behavior, and describe the situation in which the behavior occurs.* The last portion of this definition requires some elaboration. Behaviors don't occur in a vacuum. They occur in specific settings. And they occur while certain other events are also taking place. For example, a student doesn't just hit. The student hits a particular person. The student may hit during gymnastics. The student may hit only when criticized by a teacher or only when criticized by a gym instructor of the opposite sex. So describing the situation in which a behavior occurs may include where it takes place (the gym class, the playing field, or the hallway), when it takes place (morning, afternoon, lunch time), who is present (the regular teacher, a substitute teacher, a student teacher, certain other students of a class), and other seemingly incidental aspects of the situation, such as how the instruction is given (verbally or written) or whether students are shooting at a basket at a height of 6 feet rather than 7, 8, or 10 feet. The definition of that behavior would be unique because it would be defined in terms of the particular combination of circumstances that makes up the situation in which the behavior occurs. For example, one would expect a student to talk out more often with an inexperienced student teacher than with the regular teacher. Merely asking someone to observe and count the talking-out behavior of the student doesn't provide someone with a description that is sufficiently pinpointed enough to enable anyone to change the student's behavior. To pinpoint the behavior adequately one would want to count the talking-out behavior in the presence of the student teacher, assuming one wants to decrease or eliminate talking out in that situation. The more specifically one can describe the conditions surrounding the occurrence of a behavior, the more accurate the count of the behavior will be (244), and the more likely one will succeed in changing it. Look at Table 4 for some examples of pinpointing.

Describing someone as a poor loser doesn't allow anyone to recognize the behavior when it occurs, much less to count the behavior in situations where it tends to occur. But pinpointing poor loser as "hitting students after they tease him for missing a foul shot" allows anyone to observe and record this behavior. Similarly, talking about physical fitness is too vague when one is really

TABLE 4—EXAMPLES OF NON-PINPOINTED AND PINPOINTED BEHAVIORS

Non-Pinpointed Behaviors	Pinpointed Behaviors
poor loser	hits students after they tease him for missing foul shots
knowledge of rules of basketball	verbally recites differences between fouls and violations and their penalties
physical fitness	number of seconds holding the flexed-arm hang
unmotivated	percentage of required exercises performed during gym period
discipline problem	comments student makes during lecture that lead to laughter
poor baseball player	batting average

concerned with the number of seconds someone holds the flex-arm hang. A good way of deciding if a description of a behavior is adequately pinpointed is to ask yourself this question: If I were to give several people a camera and describe the behavior for them to photograph, would they all come back with the same picture? Where there are verbalizations or motion to record, substitute a tape recorder or a movie or camera for the photographic camera. Given descriptions similar to those on the left-hand portion of the above table, a number of people would without doubt all come back with different pictures, but if they were given descriptions similar to ones on the right-hand portion of the table, the pictures would be much more similar.

In physical education settings one would also want to include a criterion of acceptable performance when describing a behavior to be improved. How many push-ups one should do within a particular time period, what percentage of completed foul shots is acceptable, how fast one has to swim a lap of a pool, and what is required for the minimal length of a broad jump are examples of defining the criteria of performance. Such criteria may be specified within a curriculum, they may be reflected within physical education, athletic, and/or physical fitness norms for various standard tests (95), within particular physical fitness programs such as Cooper's aerobic training program (40), or they may be determined locally by a particular school system or teacher. Several very excellent sources describing how to pinpoint behavior in educational settings are readily available. (29,58,238) One source (244) is especially useful as a guide for writing instructional objectives based on criteria of acceptable performances that are defined with pinpointed behaviors.

Regardless of the nature of the criteria, or how they were determined, they should be made public, and the students should be told what behavior is expected of them, and what the criteria of acceptable performance are. Making pinpointed behaviors public can have a number of positive effects: Teachers and parents will know what behaviors are to be improved; they will know what is an acceptable criterion of performance; they will receive immediate positive feedback when improvements occur; and when a student's performances are continuously being evaluated against the criterion, the teaching becomes more individualized.

Describing a behavior so that anyone can see it forces everyone concerned to look at the problem out in the open, and to become aware of exactly what it is that has to be improved. This increased awareness by all concerned may be sufficient in itself to solve the problem. What were vaguely thought to be problems may not turn out to be so or may actually be different than expected. For example, a student thought to be a trouble maker actually may not talk out as much as a few others in the gym class. The student may not contribute as much as others. Merely pinpointing problems may bring this sort of thing to a teacher's attention, and it alone may solve some problems which were not previously seen too clearly. If the problem is confirmed after pinpointing, the awareness accompanying this confirmation immediately affects the way the teacher will interact with the student. In addition when the problem is described to the student in objective and pinpointed terms, the newly acquired awareness of what the teacher wants the student to do differently may result in the student attempting to improve his or her behavior by himself or herself.

Thus, simply pinpointing a behavior and describing it to those involved may be sufficient to solve the problem. If not, perhaps counting the pinpointed behavior as it occurs may help to improve it substantially.

Counting Behaviors

The second step in using the behavior modification approach successfully is counting the behavior to be improved. Counting a behavior is a continually ongoing procedure in using the behavior modification approach. As a matter of fact, it is the thing which distinguishes it from most any other technique of trying to improve behaviors. Counting behaviors both before and after a teacher applies a particular behavior modification procedure to improve a behavior will allow one to evaluate what effect the procedure is having on a student's behavior. Just counting a behavior may improve or change it. Keeping track of the number of laps swum can increase the number of laps swum (149), as can counting other behaviors in the classroom. (23) The counting makes one very aware of what is happening, and how frequently it happens. When couting by itself results in improved behavior nothing mysterious is necessarily happening. Counting a behavior after it occurs is a consequence of the behavior. Because a consequence either can have no effect at all, or can increase or decrease a behavior, counting a behavior can have no reinforcing or punishing effects whatsoever, or it can function as a reinforcement or as a punishment. Other kinds of consequences can also occur when one counts a behavior. If one shares the count with others, they may comment favorably on it. This consequence may have an additional positive effect in improving the behavior. Whether the teacher alone counts a student's behavior, or the student counts it alone, or both of them do it together, the counting gives one or both of them the kind of feedback that makes them immediately aware of what is happening and this may help to improve the behavior.

Behavior must be counted to determine acCOUNTability. Whenever anyone says they have tried the behavior modification approach but "it doesn't work," 99 out of 100 times no counting or charting had been done. Invariably the unsuccessful behavior modifiers are unaware of the technicalities of the behavioral approach and of the absolute importance of counting. Counting behaviors enables one to evaluate continually the effectiveness of the behavior modification procedures he or she might be using to change and improve a behavior. In other words, counting and charting behaviors is done for the same reason that a doctor has a patient's temperature charted, to see what's happening and to evaluate the effectiveness of the procedures the doctor is using.

There is no question that behaviors are counted by the tens of thousands in professional and amateur sports competition. The number of home runs, baskets, goals, fouls, errors, and many other statistics are being constantly accumulated and scrutinized. Those individuals whose statistics reveal improvements in behavior may become winners. The losers are those whose statistics show no improvement or worse yet, show poorer performing. Fame and fortune, and obscurity, for both players and coaches depend on these statistics. (1) The statistics which are collected in basketball (31), swimming (74), baseball (146), and other sports are often kept as charts of various kinds. These behavior counts are really tables of numbers. They represent the number of times someone hit a home run, or fouled, or the percentage of times someone may have struck out, completed a pass, etc. Athletes and students are given feedback from their coaches based on these tables, but rarely do coaches actually let their athletes have a copy of their personal progress charts. (152)

Regardless of the desirability of keeping such records, record-taking has not filtered down from the professional and amateur sports into actual ongoing physical education classes at the elementary, secondary, and even the college levels. Those who are concerned with accountability in physical education (64), and also those who are concerned with making the curriculum more objective and individualized, are very much interested in keeping good behavior records of students so that their progress can be continually evaluated. (20,108) Because behavior must be counted to determine acCOUNTability, the behavior modification approach is very compatible with the concerns of physical educators when it comes to objectively describing, counting, and continually evaluating physical education behaviors.

COUNTING TECHNIQUES

There are three interrelated classes of behaviors one might want to count in physical education settings. A number of readily available sources describe techniques for counting each of these kinds of behaviors, when counting the behaviors both of a single student and of a whole group of students. These sources describe counting techniques for physical fitness and sports behaviors (95), and various aspects of academic and social behaviors. (26,29,58,77, 241)

Most sports and physical fitness behaviors, such as someone doing a push-up, throwing a ball into a basket, hitting a triple, or lifting a weight, must be counted as they are occurring: someone must constantly be watching the person exhibiting the behavior during some set period of time. The same is true of most social behaviors, such as coming to practice on time, swearing, pushing or hitting, or saying positive things about one's athletic performance. It is important to record a behavior for a constant time each day so that the behavior counts from day to day would be comparable. Two hundred exercise behaviors during a one-hour period is not the same as one hundred in a half-hour period. When the period or allotment of time in which a behavior can occur varies from day to day, the frequency of the behavior has to be reported in terms of percentages, a way of counting very familiar to the sports world. Five home runs for five times at bat is very different from five home runs for one thousand times at bat.

Depending upon the behavior to be counted, one might record the time it took the behavior to occur, the total number of times the behavior occurred within some time period (number of swears during a 45-minute gym period, number of push-ups in 5 minutes), or the percentage of behaviors which occurred (percentage of instructions followed immediately, percentage of assigned exercises done, percentage of free throw shots completed). The kinds of sports, physical fitness, and social behaviors one would be most interested in counting are usually behaviors which quickly go on and off, a swing of a bat, a sit-up, a question asked, a push, etc. Counting behavioral events which happen, stop, then occur again as they go on and off is called event counting.

In contrast to behaviors which quickly go on and off, there are other behaviors which may appear to be either on most of the time, or off most of the time. For example, how would one record the extent to which a student is wearing glasses, sucking a thumb, or participating in a group which is engaged in some activity? In cases where a behavior can't be observed going on and off very easily, where it may be difficult to spend so much time constantly watching just to catch the occurrence of a single event, a "time sampling" counting technique can be used. The simplest way of doing this is to look at someone 10 times, every 5 or 10 minutes or so, during some set time period, a half-hour, hour, or whatever. If the individual is exhibiting the behavior of interest the moment you look at him or her, then record it as an instance of the behavior. Looking at the individual like this amounts to taking a series of still pictures, catching the person doing something at a number of different times. If a teacher looked at a student 10 times, and saw him or her participating with a group on 4 out of 10 times, then the teacher would record 40 percent group participation. A time sampling counting technique always results in the percentage of occurrence of a behavior.

Variations of this time sampling technique can be used to record the behavior of a whole group of individuals. One would record the percentage of individuals within a group who are following instructions, the percentage looking at the teacher while the teacher is talking, etc. These group time sampling procedures for counting behaviors of a whole group are discussed in more detail in the sources mentioned above. Another useful source is a recent summary of behavioral studies in the schools that deals extensively with behavior modification procedures to be used with groups of students. (86) This article can be very useful for finding out how others have gone about counting behaviors of whole groups of students, and how they have successfully used behavior modification procedures to improve these behaviors.

COUNTING DEVICES AND EQUIPMENT FOR RECORDING BEHAVIORS

Regardless of the counting technique one is using, measuring some time aspect of a behavior, the number of times it occurs, or time sampling a behavior, there are a number of different ways of actually counting and recording behaviors as they are occurring. The specific way one would count and record behaviors would be dependent upon the requirement of the particular situation. One of the simplest is to record with pencil and paper. Generally, portability and ease of use is very desirable in the selection of a recording device. One practical, portable, and flexible method of recording is to put masking tape on one's wrist and write the counts of behaviors on it. It goes where you go. Another simple way of doing this is to put objects of some sort, paper clips, coins, etc., in a pocket and move them from that pocket to another every time a behavior occurs.

Portable mechanical counters of various kinds are also available. The simplest and cheapest are the grocery counters used by shoppers in supermarkets. The counter can be used to count either one behavior, the same behavior of two different individuals, or two different behaviors of the same individual. Most of these counters have three openings. The numbers in one opening usually advances from 0 to 20, and the numbers in the remaining openings together advance from 0 to 99. A five-channel counter which can count five different behaviors of the same individual, or behaviors (same or different) for five different individuals, can be very useful in physical education settings. It fits in the palm of one's hand. (143) Golf counters can also be used for counting behaviors. (124) Bead-type counters worn on the wrist or belt (a portable abacus) can be obtained commercially (135), or can easily be made with some leather and some beads. (85)

More sophisticated kinds of counting and recording devices such as event recorders which simultaneously record the duration and frequency of 10 or 20 behaviors of the same or of different individuals are also available. (9) A number of inexpensive and portable timers (69,179) can be useful with time sampling procedures. A buzzer goes off at certain time intervals to tell the observer when to look to see if a behavior is occurring. If need be, various kinds of time-lapse photography equipment is also available. (193,194) Several very excellent and comprehensive overviews of the use of instrumentation in behavior modification (from the simplest to the most sophisticated type of equipment, including movement sensors, transducers, and radio telemetry) describe instruments which can be of immediate practical use in many physical education settings. These same sources give names and addresses of many psychological and behavior modification apparatus companies, who can provide catalogs which contain detailed descriptions of the apparatus they have available. (32,199)

GETTING STUDENTS TO COUNT BEHAVIORS

People often become overwhelmed when asked to count behaviors, probably because they haven't done it before. It may feel strange, but as with many other things one can quickly learn to do it and soon it becomes second nature. Since classrooms are full of students, it can be quite difficult to watch and count a student's behavior. It may even seem impossible to do if one wants to count several different behaviors of several different students. Although a teacher can do the counting by himself or herself there are endless other potential counters of behaviors who are just waiting to help out—the students themselves. A student can count his or her own behavior or another student's behaviors.

Few teachers take advantage of all the willing helpers there are in the classroom, although they may use older or more highly trained students to help them in class sometimes. (174) In many behavioral studies where students were asked to help teachers in implementing behavior modification procedures, students were found to be very eager to do so. (180) Letting students help the teacher in implementing the behavior modification approach may make physical education much more meaningful for them. One problem in physical education classes is that many students may have to wait around a lot, either because the classes are large or because of limited equipment or space. If students are given data sheets and counting equipment, they can count and record their own behaviors or their team's in various ways to monitor continually the performances of their classmates. Helping out in this way actively involves them in their schoolwork and provides both students and their teachers with continuous immediate feedback of their performance. Here we have a practical, inexpensive, and very effective way of providing the constant feedback and evaluation that many educators advocate as desirable in improving teaching. (20,108) With this useful feedback so readily available, teachers should be able to individualize the physical education curriculum for their students and thus help meet the specific needs of each student.

Having records of a student's progress is especially important in adaptive physical education stiuations where improvements of students are invariably uneven and slow. This kind of constant recording and evaluation of a student's progress by the teacher, the student him or herself, or by other students, will be very helpful; it will automatically show both student and teacher any small changes and improvements in a student's performance as they occur during training. The teacher will be able immediately to alter or adapt curricular materials or goals, as well as teaching procedures, so as to maximize each student's progress within his or her particular capabilities.

These kinds of behavioral records can be useful in any kind of setting, not just in regular classes or adaptive physical education settings. Teacher-, self-, or peer-monitoring can also be useful in adult physical education classes or adult physical education training. Examples of the usefulness of such records for adults in their own physical fitness programs can be found following Table 6 (p. 99).

BEHAVORIAL RECORDS FOR PARENTS

Actively involving parents in their children's education is extremely important. Behavioral improvement records are very useful for this purpose. The more detailed the information given to parents about how their children are doing in class or on an athletic team, the more positive their attitudes toward the school's physical education curriculum. The parents would also become more personally involved with the children's physical education training and support the physical education program more actively. The recent AAHPER Physical Education Division position papers for both the elementary (20), and the secondary level (108), suggested that there should be a more detailed continuous evaluation of students' performances in physical education classes than there is now. They also urged that the continuous evaluation of the student's performances be directly communicated to their parents so that they could see how well their children are doing. Unfortunately there isn't enough evaluation of students at any level of education. Most parents may get report cards of their children's progress only about four to six times a year. Furthermore, when only a letter grade is reported, it is impossible to know exactly what was happening. Sharing continuous behavioral records with parents provides them with much better feedback than the standard report card. Some schools, of course, have parent conference days where parents may come in and receive a more detailed account of their children's academic performance, but they may seldom or never provide parents the opportunity to visit their children's physical education teachers.

Many parents have negative attitudes about the physical education programs in schools. One study (119) has demonstrated that negative attitudes about physical education programs can be corrected by providing parents with information about their children's gym classes. After a slide show of the physical education classes was shown to some parents, the attitudes of these parents towards their children's physical education instruction, as measured by the Wear Physical Education Attitude Inventory, improved substantially as compared to a control group of parents who did not have this public relations experience. It's not unusual for schools to show slides of students' academic activities or exhibit students' academic projects, but these types of presentations are often similar to travelogues and may be more entertaining than informative. Most educators and parents would agree that these kinds of presentations are valuable but prefer presentations that provide more detailed information about what is going on in the schools. The continuous behavioral records advocated by the behavior modification approach supply just the kind of information parents would find most welcome. These behavioral records can supplement report cards and can be used at parent conferences to show in detail what is happening during the gym period. These records can also be taken home as frequently as desired. Keeping copies of records will preclude problems arising as a result of losing or misplacing records. Thus parents can be constantly appraised of their children's progress. Parents would then have the opportunity of commenting to their children on their progress. If the records show improvements and the parents comment favorably, then their children's performance may be enhanced even further.

Charting Behaviors

Those educators who stress the need for more continuous monitoring and evaluation of what is going on in physical education classes (20,108), and for being more accountable (64), base their arguments on either an explicit or an implicit assumption concerning the importance of feedback in improving performance. The more quantitative and qualitative feedback which can be provided to students, the better should be their performance. (217) Performance information should provide the necessary kinds of feedback to teachers who may then change their teaching procedures so as to implement the physical education curriculum more fully. There is evidence to support this assumption. In the laboratory, feedback has been demonstrated to facilitate grip strength (15), speed and accuracy of throwing (138), tennis performance (140), and other kinds of sports skills. (177) It has also been demonstrated to be very important in real-life settings. (149,186).

There is no doubt that teachers and coaches do provide feedback to improve physical fitness and athletic skills. They do it in various ways and to various degrees. One track coach merely praises an athlete for improving a previous performance and setting new personal records (92), while other coaches additionally post their athletes' performance records in track (82), swimming (74), or other sports or skills. These records, permitting comparisons of the athletes' performances from day to day, provide one kind of feedback necessary to measure progress. These records, by themselves, can be a very important motivational tool.

The kind of feedback one receives is very important. If it only amounts to verbal encouragement, and a student is told that he or she did much better than the last time, this is good. If shown a performance record for a particular day's work, this too is good. If shown a table representing a performance record for several days so that comparisons can be made, it is even better. Perhaps the best way to present feedback in physical education and athletic settings is not just verbally, or in table form, but pictorially. "A picture is worth a thousand words" is an old saying that has held up well through the years. One may show to individuals pictures of their performance: photographs of their golf swings (227), video tape recordings of their swimming (196), etc., as a way to improve some performances. An even better way of providing feedback pictorially would be to graph the performance record. The advantage of graphing physical education and athletic skills is that changes in performance can be immediately noticed, and comparisons within a given day's performances as well as comparisons among the daily performances can be made more easily. Although many coaches and teachers may keep charts of individual or group performances (31,74), they are invariably tables of statistics of one kind or another. Charting, as used in the behavior modification approach, is graphing; performance records are converted into line drawings of what someone is doing. The line graph would clearly show what was happening each day, whether it represented the percentage of curricular goals met, the number of exercises done per unit time, heights jumped, or times to perform some skill such as swimming or running.

A behavior chart (graph) is most useful when it comes to changing and improving behaviors of any kind. The most important benefit of keeping behavior charts is that they show anyone at a glance what is happening. If a line on a chart doesn't go up or down, the performance remains unchanged, even though a teacher or coach may be doing something which he or she thinks is a good idea or which the students or athletes like. The crucial question is whether or not a change in behavior is occurring. The behavior chart will show that immediately. The visual impact of a behavior chart provides an impetus to change something if the performance line on the chart isn't going up the way it should (e.g., if one is trying to improve percentage of free throw baskets, number of exercises per unit time, percentage of students on time), or down as it should (e.g., if one is trying to decrease the number of times a student swears, the percentage of errors, or the amount of time to complete a mile run). A behavior chart allows the teacher and coach as well as the student and athlete to notice very small changes in performance; many times, feedback which includes very small changes in performance may be crucial in spurring on improvements in performance. For these reasons, visual presentation of feedback is superior to that presented verbally or in tables only.

Keeping behavior charts is analogous to the keeping of medical charts. A visual graph of a patient's temperature tells a doctor at a glance what is happening to the patient's temperature and whether treatment should be changed or not. Behavior charts of a student's physical education performance serve the same function for teachers and coaches. The objective continuous records represented by a behavior chart provides teachers and coaches with the feedback needed to determine whether or not they should change their teaching procedures. Behavior charts don't lie; they tell it as it is. Nor do they make one too hopeful, or too pessimistic. If behavior charts are widely used in physical education settings, as the behavior modification approach suggests, then they will help teachers and coaches to see what is happening, and they will help them make positive changes in their teaching procedures so that their students and athletes can improve their behaviors.

A very early, and historically important, use of graphs in physical education was Howell's use of force-time graphs to train an experimental group of sprint runners how to use a rectangular foot thrust pattern with their front foot when positioning themselves on starting blocks. (90) These runners were shown graphs of their front foot pressure and were told what the ideal record should look like. Control runners received standard coaching. The runners who saw their force-time graphs performed much better than the control runners in learning to use a rectangular foot thrust pattern. In this study the runners were apparently only shown their record for the day, but not the complete records which would have enabled them to compare their daily performances. Nevertheless, the study was very successful. Unfortunately this early demonstration of the positive effects that the graphic presentation of a performance can have on an athlete did not result in the incorporation of this and similar techniques into physical education and sports training. As a matter of fact it went unnoticed. Recent behavior modification studies showing that merely keeping charts of behaviors (hand raising, out-of-seat, scratching, etc.) can change them (132), however, have begun to have some effect in physical education circles.

The public recording and sharing of feedback can be very effective in improving performance. An important component of the previously mentioned study of increasing the height of the pole vaults was having a chart of the students' performance kept in their locker room. (21) When charting changes in behavior, the changes in the charted behavior itself may function as a reinforcement or punishment. Other things may also happen to facilitate a behavior change of one kind or another. When others (students, teachers, or parents) see such a chart, they may provide verbal praise and encouragement or try to help directly.

So in some instances just keeping a graph of a student's behavior may result in changes in the behavior. In other instances just keeping a behavior chart may not result in behavior changes. In one study, having teachers count and keep charts of their verbal praises to students did not result in increasing the frequency of their praises; something else had to be done to change their behavior. (234) But regardless of whether the feedback from a chart alone helps to change a behavior, it is absolutely necessary to have such feedback from a behavior chart for two purposes. The first purpose is to allow others to see the extent to which a behavior is occurring. The second purpose is to be able to see what the behavior looks like on different days so that one can evaluate the effectiveness of any changes in teaching procedures. The behavior chart can function as a very effective method of communication. The graphic representation of a person's behavior can be easily seen and understood by others who then may be very willing to help improve the person's behavior. Figure 1, a hypothetical behavior chart, will demonstrate the importance of keeping good charts.

USING A BEHAVIOR CHART

Figure 1 shows the percentage of assigned exercises a student completed during each of two gym classes over a six-week period. In this hypothetical example a teacher was concerned about a student,

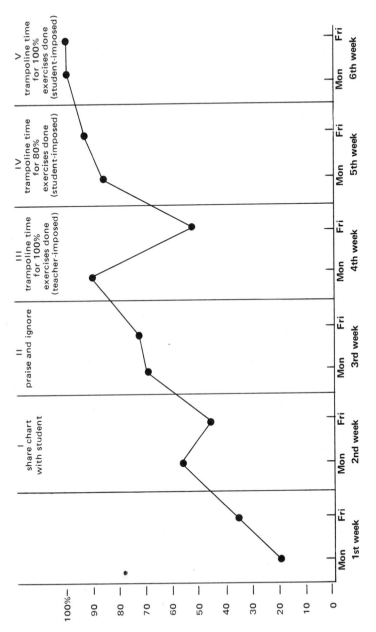

Figure 1. Percentage of Assigned Exercises Completed for Different Kinds of Change Procedures.

John, who wasn't doing all of his assigned exercises. Before beginning to use the behavior modification approach for improving some behavior, the frequency of occurrence of the behavior must first be counted for around a week. This week of "before" or "baseline" counting provides the teacher with a basis for comparing how well a behavior modification procedure actually works. It's like a doctor taking your blood pressure or temperature a few times before doing something to try to improve it. John's teacher kept a record of the percentage of exercises he did during the week of baseline counting and made a chart of it. As you can see, John's exercising increased from around 20 percent to 35 percent of the assigned exercises. This improvement could very well have been due to the teacher's counting John's exercising. The phenomena of seeing a behavior improve in some way during this baseline phase isn't unusual, and, as has been mentioned, counting a behavior alone may sometimes result in the behavior becoming entirely improved.

The first procedure for John's teacher was to show John the chart of his performance each day. He told him that he expected 100 percent of his assigned exercises to be done each day, and he told him that he would show him his performance on the behavior chart. The teacher did this for the next two gym periods, and praised him for his performance when he showed him the chart. John's exercising jumped up to around 55 percent on the first day, but dropped down to around 45 percent on the second day. Showing John the behavior chart was initially somewhat effective, but it wasn't permanent, nor was it as effective as his teacher wanted it to be.

When a behavior change procedure doesn't work as well as it should after consistently using it for a week, what a teacher was doing should be analyzed and changed and improved upon in some fashion. When the teacher thought of what he could do to make things go better, he asked himself, "What do I do when John is exercising? Do I ignore him? What do I do when I catch him not exercising, and kidding around with the other students? Do I criticize him?" When the teacher reflected on these questions, he quickly realized that he was constantly telling John to get back to his exercising when he was kidding around, but that he almost never went over to him and said anything nice to him when he was exercising. He was inadvertently "catching John being bad," and ignoring him when he was being good. He made an effort to try to "catch John being good" more often when he was exercising, and tried to praise him at least four or five times during each gym period. When he saw John goofing off, the teacher turned his back on him to ignore him (and instead of yelling at John, he found someone else doing his or her work and praised that student instead of criticizing John). He told John that he still expected 100 percent of his exercises to be done each day, and he continued to show him his behavior chart, and praised him for his performance when he showed him the chart. You can see from the behavior chart during the second phase that praising John during the gym period, in addition to showing him the chart and praising him at the end of the day, increased his exercising to around 70 percent of his assigned exercises.

The teacher decided to use a different procedure during the fourth week. He knew John liked to use the trampoline since he used it whenever he could; so he told him that if he did 100 percent of his exercises, he could use if for the last five minutes of each gym period. John complained that the teacher was expecting too much of him, and that he couldn't do 100 percent of his exercises right away. The teacher didn't give in, and John agreed to try. On the first day he did 90 percent of his assigned exercises but complained that it was a lot of work. On the the second day his performance dropped to around 50 percent. John never earned the chance to go on the trampoline. The procedure almost worked, but almost doesn't count, and it antagonized John in the process.

The teacher began to analyze what may have gone wrong this time. He soon realized that he had been unilaterally imposing the 100 percent criterion of performance on John for the previous three weeks, and that this may have been somewhat unfair. He wondered what would happen if John could determine what percentage of the exercises he had to do in order to use the trampoline. He discussed this with John. John said that he would like to do 80 percent of his assigned exercises. The teacher thought this was a little too low, but, as you can see, John did 85 percent of them on Monday and 90 percent of them on Friday of that fourth week. During the sixth week the teacher again asked him what criterion he wanted to set for himself. John said 100 percent, and as the behavior chart shows he met this self-imposed criterion during both gym periods of that week.

As this hypothetical example shows, keeping a behavior chart provides both a teacher and student with immediate feedback. It show both successes and failures, and it helps in guiding them to finding better solutions to their problems. It should be mentioned that a general tactic which should be used in any behavior improvement project is to invite students, or others involved in it, to participate actively in setting up and conducting the project. They should be asked to help in determining what the problem may be (pinpointing), what the goals should be, the criterion of performance, and the procedures to use in attaining these goals. Research shows that the performance of students is much better when this is done, than when all of this imposed upon them. (127)

GETTING STUDENTS TO CHART BEHAVIORS

It is reasonable to assume that if every student in physical education classes had behavior charts of his or her performances, then this alone would positively affect the physical fitness and athletic abilities of literally thousands of individuals. The behavior modification approach advocates that this be done. But who is going to make up and keep all of these behavior charts current? The answer, of course, is the students themselves. Teachers who are already using the behavior modification approach have their students keeping behavior charts of their performances. Students keep their own, or other students help them to do this. Even kindergarten children can keep such charts, and they are especially useful in adaptive physical education settings. Students don't even have to be able to read to understand behavior charts. All that any student needs to know is that if the line on a chart is going up (or down) things are going well, depending upon what behavior is being improved by increase or decrease.

Students can be easily taught to keep such charts, and most students enjoy doing this a great deal. Each student can have his or her own manila file folder to keep as many behavior improvement charts in it as need be for his or her particular needs. Students can keep a copy of their charts with them at all times, they can look at them as often as they want to, and they can show them to their friends or parents as they choose. These kinds of daily behavior charts provide students with constant feedback for their performance. They know exactly where they are each day, and they know exactly how far they yet have to go to complete a particular aspect of their training which may be represented on one of their behavior charts. These kinds of charts show both students and their parents what is going on in the gym. They vividly show improvement in behaviors and they serve to improve public relations with parents, with others in the schools, and with the community. Behavior charts provide individualized progress charts for each student and can be very useful for individualizing the curriculum for each student. Each student would be expected to improve at his or her own rate, and each student's chart would be used by a teacher to help design a program to meet his or her own individual needs.

There are a number of useful sources which discuss charting behaviors. (26,27,100,151) In addition to published research reports in behavior modification or books on behavior modification, a highly useful and readily accessible source for teachers on both counting and charting behaviors is a booklet in a very good series on behavior modification. (77) Another booklet in this series has numerous examples of behavior charts and projects summarized in a fashion that would appeal to teachers. It offers concrete examples of how the behavior modification approach has been used by teachers in their classrooms (and by parents at home), and provides models for do-it-yourself projects. (78)

Behavior Modification as Applied Experimentation

Using the behavior modification approach in the gymnasium amounts to the running of an applied experiment. A physical education teacher would be performing an applied experiment when he or she systematically applies a particular teaching procedure (independent variable) in order to improve some behavior (dependent variable) of a student or a group of students. Because experiments can be done using any behavior as a dependent variable and any teaching procedure as an independent variable, in any kind of setting, this experimental approach to evaluating teaching effectiveness has unlimited applications in physical education settings. Doing behavior modification experiments provides a teacher with the flexibility to try out any kind of innovative procedures on any student behavior. Furthermore, one would get a clear-cut record of what is happening since one would objectively define the behaviors serving as dependent variables, and objectively define and systematically manipulate the teaching procedures serving as independent variables. The hypothetical example of John's exercising behavior as a dependent variable illustrates how to manipulate systematically a number of independent variables in order to get an improvement in a dependent variable. The experimental approach provides a built-in evaluation procedure which allows a teacher or anyone else to compare before and after performances on a behavior chart. The teacher may then use self-correcting tactics when things aren't going the way they should be.

A dependent variable is defined as any measurable aspect of a behavior. A physical education teacher may want to change the time it takes someone to run a mile, the number of sit-ups done in five minutes, the percentage of assignments done by a particular student, the number of verbal contributions a student makes in class, or the percentage of all of the students in a class who complete their assignments. All of these are measurable aspects of students' behaviors. An independent variable is defined as any event which is systematically changed or manipulated in some fashion. One would select an independent variable that is expected to result in some sort of positive change in the student's behavior that was selected as the dependent variable. One might change the temperature in a room, the buoyancy of water wings, the height of a basketball net, the number of substeps in teaching some skill, how often one praises students, when one praises students, how often one criticizes students, allowing students to miss a practice if they meet a certain level of performance during soccer practice, etc. Each of these events can be systematically changed in some way by a teacher. A teacher can increase his or her praises from 10 to 30 during a gym period, or he or she can vary the amount of air in water wings.

The most important source of independent variables which is likely (positively or negatively) to affect students' behaviors in their physical education classes is the teacher. Teachers can arrange the teaching environment in endless ways, and they can arrange their own behavior, both before (as antecedents), and after (as conse-

TABLE 5—EXAMPLES OF INDEPENDENT AND DEPENDENT VARIABLES IN PHYSICAL EDUCATION SETTINGS

Independent Variable	Dependent Variable
send child to homeroom	number of sassing remarks
self-record laps swum	number of laps swum
miss track practice	height of pole vault
sit-down commands	number of students standing up
tokens	number of revolutions of exercise bicycle
public scolding of athlete	number of athletic errors made

quences) their students do something. Basically teachers are walking, talking, independent variables. In fact, a great deal of the work dealing with the application of behavior modification to educational settings has concentrated on trying to demonstrate experimentally the ways a teacher's behaviors can function as important independent variables that increase or decrease their students' behaviors. Some examples of independent and dependent variables in physical education settings are given in Table 5.

In the hypothetical case of Susan, where the teacher consistently sent her back to her homeroom every time Susan sassed him, we have the basic ingredients of an applied experiment with the teacher as the talking independent variable. The teacher could systematically vary the independent variable, either sending Susan back to her room or ignoring her, and compare the frequency of Susan's sassing under each experimental condition. Systematic changes in the independent variables, self-recording of laps swum (149), missing track practice (21), sit-downs commands (131), and receiving tokens for exercising (123), have been shown to change the corresponding dependent variable (see Table 5).

As has been mentioned, one of the problems with the advice given in many athletic and physical education magazines and journals is that it isn't specific enough. The variables they might want others to change aren't described clearly, nor are many other important aspects of the situation clarified, and because of this fact alone the advice isn't too useful. In one such article it was suggested that scolding a particular athlete so that it would anger him would lead to a reduction of errors. (218) Translated into a workable hypothesis, into experimental language, the author suggests that scolding, an independent variable, will reduce errors, a dependent variable. Even so the author doesn't indicate whether the scolding is given privately or in public, the extent to which the athlete is criticized, etc. Once the exact way one should go about scolding is defined, then one can easily conduct an experiment to see whether scolding (as defined) does in fact have the suggested effect on athletic errors.

From an experimental viewpoint, pinpointing and counting behaviors amount to defining and measuring dependent variables. And using any kind of a behavior modification procedure amounts to applying an independent variable in a particular situation. The continuous behavior charts a teacher keeps enables him or her to see how the dependent variable (plotted on the vertical line—the ordinate) changes when independent variables are introduced. There are many technical problems in conducting any experiment, but particularly so in using the behavior modification approach in applied settings. The most common problems are demonstrating the reliability of the chosen measurement of the behavior to be changed and adequately demonstrating that the independent variables manipulated did, in fact, produce the changes one observes (problems of control). The rationale for using behavior modification procedures in real-life settings (7,17,213), and the technicalities of experimentally performing such studies (44,107,180, 230) are discussed in a number of readily available sources.

BEHAVIOR MODIFICATION CHANGE PROCEDURES

There are a variety of behavior modification techniques for improving behaviors. Each of them, in essence, are different independent variables which may be used separately or in combination with others to try to change and improve students' behaviors, the dependent variable of interest to teachers. There are two basic problems facing teachers in physical education settings. The first problem is helping a student develop a new behavior, one that he or she isn't exhibiting up to the standards he or she should, or one that he or she isn't exhibiting at all—such as getting an extremely slow jogger to jog a mile in 15 minutes rather than 30 minutes, or getting someone who is afraid of entering the water to lie prone in the water. The second problem is keeping a behavior going, maintaining it at a particular level once it is developed, or improving it to an optimal level. In both instances one would want to provide appropriate consequences for these behaviors such as praise, free time activities, prizes, or whatever. A short discussion of two important procedures for helping students to develop new complex motor or social skills will first be presented, and then a discussion of social reinforcement techniques for maintaining and improving behaviors will follow.

Procedures for Developing New Behaviors

SHAPING PROCEDURES

One teaching procedure everyone uses without knowing its technical term or the behavioral principle on which it is based is *shaping*. When a coach consistently praises swimmers every time they swim a little faster than the last time and every time they break their own personal record, he's using a shaping procedure. (92) Shaping is defined as reinforcing successively closer and closer approximations to a desired behavior. It is a more refined version of the procedure used by children to help someone find a hidden object by saying "You're getting warmer" each time they move closer to the hidden object. When teachers structure a learning situation so that they don't expect too much too quickly from their students, they are using a variation of the shaping procedure. Many of the physical fitness and athletic skills they want to develop in their students are only in the formative stages. A teacher's task is to take each student from where he or she happens to be and develop his or her behavior to some acceptable level of performance. Coaching and athletic magazines and journals yield numerous anecdotal examples of using step-by-step procedures to take students from one level of performance to a much higher level, in fencing (209) and in weight lifting (200), to mention but two examples. Shaping can even be used to individualize a whole curriculum by breaking it into a number of sequential substeps for students to master. (76)

One of the suggestions of the AAHPER position papers on physical education (20,108) was that there should be a much more systematic sequential development of physical education skills. From a behavioral viewpoint the position papers are advocating using shaping procedures as are those who promote individualized instruction in physical education. (76) Having clear-cut behavioral subgoals for students to master step-by-step has many advantages for both students and teachers. Teachers would be able to individualize programs much more easily and to state their behavioral goals more specifically. Students would know exactly where they are and what they have to do on any particular day in order to progress towards their goal. (200) And if daily behavioral records are kept for each student, then the student's rate of progress could be determined. These records could be taken home and shown to parents, as one advocate of individualized instruction in physical education has suggested. (76) The behavior modification approach would go further and require the charting of records so that changes in performance, including those small changes easily missed, are more readily apparent. Using shaping procedures also helps to protect students from teachers who expect too much of them and are demanding, as was John's teacher who demanded that he do 100 percent of the exercises, instead of using a shaping procedure (which was discussed in the section on charting). In fact, shaping procedures provide both teachers and students with the patience to develop complex behaviors. Finally it helps everyone reach his or her goals, some more slowly than others.

There are a number of interesting examples of how useful shaping procedures can be to physical education teachers. These procedures have been used to get children to approach and use outdoor play equipment. (30,79,97) They have also been used to get geriatric patients to take longer walks, increasing the length of the walk from a few minutes to 15 minutes or so a day (190), and to get a mentally retarded *spina bifida* child to use crutches by using a 10-step training program. (89) Suggestions have been made for the more intentional use of shaping procedures in teaching swimming. (186) A 6-step program has been used to teach handicapped students the sidestroke and the backstroke. (70) A 16-step shaping procedure has been used to get 5- to 12-year-old children into the water (122), and a 26-step shaping program has been used to get 17- to 19-year-olds to do the same thing. (204)

A very important example of an application of shaping procedures is Cooper's aerobic training program. (40) Cooper has incorporated a number of behavioral principles and procedures into his program without labeling or perhaps even recognizing them as such. His program is individually tailored for people of different ages and provides a number of tables of prescriptions of different exercise programs for the various age groups. Each table consists of graduated exercise goals which guide the user in gradually increasing the extent of their exercising while simultaneously gradually decreasing the time to do this, thus increasing one's aerobic (heart, lung) capacity. Cooper himself refers to his program as a progressive exercise technique and states that he considers this progression to be the key to the program. The program has been structured so that the individual who follows it will expend the necessary amount of energy to develop adequate heart and lung capacity. Cooper's tables list points which an individual would earn on completing any particular step of the program. A total of 30 points a week, which can be obtained in a wide variety of ways, is necessary to meet an adequate standard of aerobic capacity. (The points attributed to the various activities were determined by careful laboratory experiments.) Keeping track of the number of points one gets for various kinds of different exercise or sports activities allows one to combine their effects and monitor his or her own progress. Keeping track of the number of points one earns each day provides an individual with constant feedback for the particular program. Cooper has made the observation. "Here lies the unique merit of the aerobic system: you can measure your own progress. . . ." (40:17) Cooper's aerobic program is such an excellent application of shaping procedures that the behavior modification approach would offer only a minor (but useful) suggestion for improving the program—keeping a pictorial chart of the daily points one earns instead of just writing them down on a piece of paper.

Cooper's aerobic program has been used in combination with a token system to help a young woman jog more each day. (101) The program has also been used with almost 800 junior high school students. (41) These students increased the distance they could run in Cooper's 12-minute test by 17.7 percent after following his program. In contrast, a control group of students who took regular gym classes made no improvement at all from the pre-test to the post-test. Here we have an example of the large scale applicability of a behavioral shaping precedure. If Cooper's program and shaping procedures in general were more widely used in physical education and exercise training, it is quite conceivable that the health of the nation would be improved substantially.

The systematic use of shaping procedures in physical education settings has a number of important advantages to offer. The procedures inform students of the desired goal, allowing them to keep track of their own progress and to see what remains to reach the goal. Not knowing where one is going, how far one has gone, or how far one yet has to go is a state of affairs no one wants. Another advantage of using shaping procedures more systematically, and making the steps public, is that anyone can pick up where one teacher left off, the teacher in the next grade or school, a substitute teacher, or even a parent or student. Knowing what is expected of him or her, and what the next steps are, students would become more actively engaged in their physical education training. Using shaping procedures teaches everyone involved a very important lesson: with patience, even the most difficult behaviors can be learned. Shaping can best be remembered as simply, "little steps for little feet."

PROMPTING–FADING PROCEDURES

A second type of teaching procedure commonly used in physical education settings without knowing its technical name or the underlying behavioral principle is *prompting-fading*. Whenever a teacher gives a student any kind of physical help or guidance in performing some task, the teacher is prompting a behavior to occur. Positioning a student's body in some way is one example, standing behind someone and helping him or her swing a golf club or a baseball bat is another. Holding a student in the water so that he or she doesn't sink is a prompting procedure, as is holding a two-wheeled bicycle so that a child can ride it. Prompting is defined as any antecedent event which helps to start a behavior. A prompt can be any kind of an event, a verbalization, actual physical guidance, some sort of cue, or even some physical device which helps a behavior to occur. An inflection of one's voice can be used as a prompt to get a behavior going, "Begin on the count of three: one, two, THREE!"

At the lower grades physical education teachers encounter students who don't know left from right. In trying to teach them left from right they often meet with failure, and a typical way of resolving this problem is to do nothing, attribute the failure to their "age," "level of maturation," "perceptual awareness," or "lack of appropriate cognitive development." A prompting-fading procedure, however, can turn such failures into successes long before the students mature. Just put a big circle on the student's right hand with a marking pen (or a piece of masking tape, or a ribbon). Now the students always will know which is their right hand. With appropriate practice the penned circle should be gradually made smaller and smaller (faded) while the student continues to retain the learned behavior, until the prompt is completely taken away and the student can tell left and right without the help of the prompt. Any student, even those in adaptive physical education, will learn left from right, and almost immediately. To handle problems of the mirror image the teacher would put a mark (prompt) on his or her own right hand.

Various kinds of physical devices already are functioning as prompts in physical education settings. A commercially available device consisting of a pair of collars that positions one's wrist and the putter in the proper position are used by golfers to facilitate a pendulum-like arc in their putting. The safety harnesses used by gymnasts on the trampoline, balance beam, and for floor exercises is another example of a physical prompting device, as are water wings and other kinds of flotation devices.

The goal in physical education training is to get students eventually to perform various behaviors and sports skills without assistance. Therefore a teacher would want to decrease gradually the extent to which assistance is given in holding a golf club or baseball bat, keeping afloat in the water, or working out on a balance beam. Doing so is equivalent to using a fading procedure. Fading is defined as the *gradual removal of a prompt*. It amounts to withdrawing whatever kinds of assistance or guidance were initially used to help start a behavior.

Prompting-fading procedures are used when a student can't exhibit a behavior by himself or herself. It's important that the assistance given a student is gradually withdrawn (faded). If the withdrawing of support is too abrupt then a student may become upset, and even fail. To avoid abrupt fading, the physical education skills or sports skills can be divided arbitrarily into a number of levels to coincide with the same number of fading levels. Then as a student progresses to the next level of the physical education or sports skill his or her prompt will automatically by reduced to the appropriate fading level. When gradual fading becomes a standard training procedure in physical education, then students can see the extent of their progress as prompts are systematically faded. This progress can be visually shown to students on charts, and both teacher and student will know exactly what is happening.

When students are given lighter or modified sports equipment a prompting procedure is being used. (250) Problems can arise if students continually use modified equipment. They may become overtrained on it and may not perform as well as they should when they have to use standard equipment. If the equipment in the major kinds of sports and physical fitness activities were graduated in weight (or some other relevant attribute), then students could begin with the weight level that felt comfortable and afforded them some success. As their performance progressed, they would gradually replace their equipment with a heavier model until they could perform adequately using standard equipment. Water wings and other kinds of flotation devices used in teaching swimming could be adapted in this way for the purpose of fading the support they give to swimmers. Although it has been demonstrated that it is more effective to teach swimming with water wings than without them, these prompts are usually removed very abruptly. (102) It should be much more efficient, and effective, to use a number of water wings with different degrees of buoyancy. Students could then use the water wings in order, progressing from the most buoyant to the least buoyant, gradually learning to swim more and more under their own power.

Along with shaping and prompting-fading procedures teachers often use demonstrations to teach new behaviors. This method amounts to a modeling or imitation procedure. It too is a very important teaching tool. However, it has not been explored as much in physical education settings as it has in other areas. (10) A very useful manual on the use of imitation in educational settings is available. (219) Several general discussions of the use of shaping and prompting-fading and also available (13,33,151): one deals specifically with physical education. (189) A number of sources are especially useful because they have step-by-step detailed programs (with pictures) of shaping, prompting-fading, and imitation procedures for teaching a variety of behaviors (167,242,243); one of these would be most useful in teaching sports and recreational behaviors. (242) Although the procedures discussed in these sources deal with their applications to handicapped and retarded individuals, the general principles and procedures are applicable to individuals of all kinds, and all ages, and in any setting.

Procedures for Increasing and Decreasing Behaviors

There are a variety of consequences which may function to increase or decrease behaviors. Verbal praise is one such consequence; it frequently functions as a reinforcement. Consequently, social reinforcement procedures are the most important procedures anyone can use to improve any behavior. Teachers should always use social reinforcement procedures, either alone or in addition to other procedures for increasing behaviors, such as activity or token reinforcement procedures. They should also always use social reinforcement procedures when they use a punishment procedure to decrease some inappropriate behavior. If one were to observe teachers who are very successful in teaching physical education skills, one would find them lavishly praising their students. Behavior modification research has gone beyond simple observation and looked into the complexities of social reinforcement to show us how to use it most effectively. The single most important procedure a physical education teacher could learn from the behavior modification approach is how best to use verbal praise as social reinforcement.

SOCIAL REINFORCEMENT PROCEDURES

All teachers are very much interested in how to motivate students. They are curious about what some teachers do that makes them more effective than others. This concern is reflected in physical education articles appearing in both coaching and research-oriented journals. The focus of interest is the teacher's behaviors, primarily verbal behaviors. The nice things teachers say are thought to be of crucial importance in teaching. Articles from coaching journals urge teachers to use "verbal incentives" (218), and to "always encourage, and never discourage." (236) They suggest that verbal praise is the most common form of positive motivation (118), that one should verbally praise students as much as possible, even "brag" about them (92), and that one should "never miss opportunities to praise someone for a good performance." (232) Although the authors of these and many other articles of this type don't offer any concrete evidence for their opinions, behavioral studies in the schools have found it very good advice. These authors also offer other kinds of advice, such as advocating "scolding" (218), or saying that "too much praise can weaken its effect," or that a "blend of criticism and praise" tailored to each student's needs can be beneficial to him or her (232) for which no evidence has been found.

After it was suggested that physical educators should spend more time descriptively studying teacher–student interactions (4), a number of individuals developed a variety of ways of doing so. (66,159,198,248) Unfortunately, each investigator developed a separate category system, with a distinct terminology and particular descriptions of what constitutes each category of behavior. In fact, the investigators have pinpointed similar sounding behaviors in different ways in some instances, and in other instances they haven't given adequate behavioral descriptions of behaviors. Consequently, it is difficult to compare results obtained from these different systems. One study relating the climate of a class (supportive or defensive) with teacher behaviors rated actual teacher behaviors according to whether they were "positive emotive behaviors" or "negative emotive behaviors." These gross behavioral categorizations were compared with the results obtained from using other kinds of category systems to study teacher behaviors in the classroom. An examination of these behavioral categories (19: 344–5) shows that the common terms used to describe positive emotive teacher behaviors are *approval, reassurance, praise, encourage, supportive behavior, shows affective behaviors;* and the common terms to describe negative emotive teacher behaviors are *behavioral disapproval, deprecating students, criticisms, justifies authority, uses sarcasm, threatens,* or *reproves.* These two broad classes of teacher verbal behaviors identified in these varied educational studies are roughly comparable to the more general terms *teacher verbal praise* and *teacher verbal criticism.*

Although both the anecdotal advice and the results of descriptive studies of teachers' verbal interactions with students emphasize the importance of a teacher's praise and criticism, neither actually demonstrates it: they don't show a functional relationship between praising and criticizing and a student's academic or social performance. Behavior modification studies in the schools repeatedly demonstrate that a teacher's verbal praises and criticisms are very important independent variables which affect students' behaviors for better and for worse. Using verbal praise alone can improve a student's behaviors in nursery grades (2), elementary (81), or high school. (144) Verbal praise can improve a child's walking (83), the walking of geriatric patients (190), and the extent to which normal (30,97), or brain injured children use monkey bars or climbing frames (79). These and other studies on using verbal praise in the classroom also offer physical education teachers very specific advice on exactly how to change their praising and criticizing in order to more effectively generate desirable academic and/or social behaviors in their students.

Before considering this experimental evidence and its implications for helping to implement the physical education curriculum, consider some real-life situations and you will see that social consequences are very important for all of us. Students interact quite differently with their own teachers as compared with substitute teachers, or with other teachers in their school setting. They may be devils with one teacher and angels with others, all within a matter of a few minutes. The same thing happens at home. Children may behave very well with baby sitters or grandparents but fight and produce problems with their parents. Conversely, they may cause all sorts of commotion and problems for the sitters or grandparents, but be very good with their parents. In other words, children seem to behave in different ways depending upon whom they are with. These kinds of common anecdotal observations suggest strongly that what goes on between children and adults, especially in terms of the consequences adults provide for children, is very important. Behavior modification experiments in the school, home, and other settings show that a functional relationship between social consequences and behavior does exist.

A variety of social consequences, praising, complimenting, smiling, patting on the head (even frowning, and criticizing), have been shown to increase a variety of children's and adults' behaviors. When these or any other kinds of social consequences (even spanking a child) are shown to increase the frequency of a behavior that follow, they are, technically, social reinforcements. A social reinforcement is defined as *any social consequence of a behavior which increases the occurrence of the behavior in the future.* So a social reinforcement is a social event which follows a behavior and increases the frequency of that behavior. Social consequences supplied by nursery school teachers (25), elementary school teachers (81,130, 226), high school teachers (144), and, yes, principals (42) have all been demonstrated to function as social reinforcement for students. Children can even provide social consequences that improve their teacher's behaviors. (45) Praise can also be very effective when used by parents at home to help improve school-related behaviors (79,237). Any teacher consequence, regardless of what it is, even scolding, might function as a social reinforcement. It is important to keep good data and charts in order to determine if a particular social consequence does, indeed, function as a social reinforcement and to identify those social consequences that generally work as social reinforcements. Keeping good records of what is happening allows one to see what effects a change in a teacher's behavior is having on his or her students. Without records one can't tell what is happening, and one may be easily deceived. Maybe a teacher's scolding does improve a student's behavior, maybe not. Without records we might think the scolding works: but if a chart shows that the frequency of hitting by a student increases when the teacher scolds (as compared to hitting behavior without the scolding), then we know otherwise. Behavioral records and charts can't deceive us.

Classroom Discipline and Social Reinforcement

Some teachers may spend a great deal of time just repeating instructions and going over the rules again and again. Instructions are a form of antecedent events which are given in the hope that they will make certain behaviors occur. When students don't follow instructions or rules, teachers may wonder why. The teachers may not have provided students with appropriate consequences whenever they did follow the instructions. (16) The relative effectiveness of simply reciting classroom rules, merely ignoring inappropriate behaviors, and praising students for appropriate behaviors have been experimentally analyzed in a number of recent studies. (79,81,178) Simply reciting the rules to students was found not to be very effective. Merely ignoring unwanted behaviors (and not doing anything else) was also found ineffective. Praising students for their performance was found to be most effective in attaining classroom control. Once a teacher becomes aware of what he or she is actually doing in the classroom, and how to use praise and criticism more effectively, then students' behaviors can improve very significantly.

Numerous behavioral studies have shown that teachers unknowingly, and accidentally, produce many of the behavioral discipline problems they have with their students. A general finding is that when teachers' verbal criticisms exceed their verbal praises to a certain degree, a student, several students, or a whole class can go out of control. The study mentioned earlier, dealing with sit-down commands, dramatically illustrates this phenomenon. When teachers increased their sit-down commands (in an effort to have more students seated), more students stood up. When they reduced their sit-down commands to very few, fewer students stood up. But when they reduced their sit-down commands to zero (consistently ignoring those standing up) and simultaneously praised other students as they were sitting (something they never did before), fewer students were standing up than ever before. (131) This study demonstrated that a large number of teacher verbal criticisms combined with fewer verbal praises actually functioned as a social reinforcement and produced discipline problems in the class. This same phenomenon was also demonstrated in a class which initially was in perfect control. When the teacher systematically increased the number of times she criticized the class while simultaneously reducing the number of times she praised the class, the class went out of control. (226) The lesson these and other studies demonstrate should be self-evident.

Teacher criticisms can also have detrimental effects on academic performances of various kinds. A recent study has shown that talking to children about the digit reversals they make actually increases these kinds of errors. (84) Teachers have always corrected errors of one sort or another, and on the basis of various behavioral studies one may begin to wonder what good (or bad) it may have been doing. One may also begin to wonder if it is better to put big X's through a student's errors, or is it better to leave the mistakes unmarked and merely put big C's through the correct answers on a student's paper?

Observations of literally thousands of teachers have shown that where things aren't going well teachers criticize much more often than they praise. They criticize around four to five times more than they praise. (133) One recent observational study of the relative verbal praise and criticism rates of teachers from a number of grade levels showed that up to the second grade teachers dispensed more praises than criticisms to their students. Beyond the second grade teachers on the average dispensed more verbal criticisms than praises to their students. (245) Assuming that these findings would hold true throughout the country, then there should be great concern over this matter. Evidence from a variety of other sources suggests that this phenomenon may, indeed, be quite universal, not only in the schools but in institutions (71,240), and the home (96, 247) as well.

Teachers in physical education classes may also criticize more than they praise. At least one study, of 40 physical education teachers at the upper elementary, high school, and college level, showed that 333 teacher verbalizations were criticisms or statements justifying authority, while only 94 verbalizations were praise or encouragement. Of the thousands of verbalizations which were recorded from these teachers (12,620), they were criticizing 2.6 percent of the time while praising only .7 percent. They were producing around 4 criticisms for every verbal praise. (159) Considering the total number of students these 40 teachers were teaching, one can only conclude that very few were getting praised by their teachers. Students should be caught more often being good (and praised) than being bad (and criticized).

Safety in the Gym and Social Reinforcement

Recognizing that adverse effects can occur when one criticizes and complains more often than when one praises and compliments, teachers could apply this knowledge to prevent numerous problems they encounter in the classroom or gymnasium. Consider the problem of physical safety. One estimate of the frequency of school accidents is that around 50 percent of them occur during physical education training, and that 65 percent of these occur during class instructional periods. For this reason physical education teachers are urged to be more concerned with safety education, both while in college and as a practicing physical education teacher. (54) What kind of training should physical education teachers get so that they can prevent more accidents in the gymnasium? What can a teacher do to decrease the possibility of accidents in the gym classes?

A behavioral analysis of the safety problem would involve look-ing for possible antecedents and consequences of accidents. It is conceivable that attending and criticizing inappropriate and dan-gerous behaviors in a gymnasium may actually increase them. On the other hand, if students are praised whenever they exhibit "safe" behaviors during gym class, these safe behaviors should, most probably, increase in frequency (and preclude the occurrence of an accident). How often does the average physical education teacher praise students when they perform in an appropriate and safe man-ner? Perhaps each teacher should set a goal of praising each day at least 10 different students in each gym class for doing something in a safe manner. The students will continually be reminded to perform safely and everyone will be eventually praised. Such a tactic can only produce positive results.

How to Make Verbal Praise More Effective with Students

If a number of specific suggestions, based on behavior modification research done in the schools, were incorporated by physical educa-tion teachers into their teaching methods, they could maximize their teaching effectiveness with their students. These specific sug-gestions are all aimed at enhancing the extent to which a teacher's verbal praises can function as social reinforcements for their students. Each of them is based upon what other teachers have done, and each has been experimentally demonstrated to be effec-tive. Each suggestion should help to increase the number of times a teacher positively interacts with each student. The general lesson for any teacher to learn from these suggestions is to *minimize the criticism, and raise the praise!* More specifically:

　　1. *Keep a daily count and chart of verbal praises given to individual children* (do not include class praise) for at least one-half hour a day, preferably during an instructional period. One need not count verbal criticisms, unless so desired. Increase the praise rate to at least one time every two minutes on the average (15 per half-hour, 30 per hour, 150–180 per day). If this rate has already been reached, increase praising as much as possible. (29) Count-ing one's own verbal praises and charting them each day will make a teacher very much aware of his or her praising behavior. For many teachers, just seeing this feedback and knowing a

specific goal to attain will be sufficient to increase their verbal praise. The others may have to appeal to someone else, a spouse, perhaps, to provide additional consequences (a special meal, being taken out to dinner, being allowed to skip a household chore, etc.) for successfully increasing the rate of praising. If necessary one could provide consequences (a movie, weekend trip, a book, etc.) oneself.

2. *Praise students about equally.* Both casual and systematic observation of the classroom show that many students don't receive their fair share of teacher attention. In lower grades teachers may ask their students to keep track of the teacher's praises by tallying them on cards. Moving around the classroom or gym, the teacher can see if the praises and compliments are being distributed about equally. For older children, and adult students, the teacher could keep track of this distribution of praises on a piece of paper, or arbitrarily divide the class into subgroups and make sure that each member of a subgroup is praised before going on to the next subgroup (192), or give students tokens for their performance. (139) In the token procedure, the token serves as a cue for the teacher to praise the student each time a token is given. If each student would receive only a certain number of tokens during each gym period, it will insure that the teacher praises each class member equally. There are other ways to aid a teacher in dispensing praise equally among students. (29)

3. *Praise the student's behaviors as well as the student.* Praise should be descriptive. Mentioning the behavior one is praising, e.g., "You had a much smoother transition this time with your left leg extension during your turn into stage front," should be more effective in increasing that particular behavior of a dancer than merely saying, "I liked the way you did it this time a lot better." Behavioral research has shown that descriptive verbal praise is more effective in generating various kinds of behaviors than nondescriptive praise. (67,73) It has been suggested that providing performance information along with positive evaluative comments may be one of the most important tasks of a physical educator. (248) And yet observational studies of physical education teachers have shown that teachers don't mention behaviors very often when they praise. They tend to use repetitive patterns of words, in many cases, the same words, and often words only remotely related to a student's specific performance. (66) Although feedback accounted for a major portion of teacher verbalizations to students in another study, most often the teachers' verbalizations were quite neutral and redundant, such as saying "okay" and "all right." (198) A recent study of teaching handicapped children how to

swim has demonstrated that task-specific praise plus corrections was much more effective in teaching them to swim than was non–task-specific praise. (70)

4. *Ignore inappropriate behaviors* unless they are dangerous, or extremely disruptive to others. A teacher always has the choice of catching one student being bad, or catching another student being good at any given moment in a class. The time which is spent criticizing one student for being bad can always be spent praising another student for being good. Rather than fuss about a student doing something annoying, find another student whose performance could be praised. Knowing the effects praise and criticism can have on children's behaviors, the choice a teacher should make in such situations should be quite clear. (84,130,131) A teacher can be aided in ignoring a student's behavior by turning his or her back on the student and finding another student behaving appropriately and praising him or her.

5. *Maintain a 5:1 praise/criticism ratio.* As mentioned earlier, teachers criticize more than they praise (around four or five criticisms per praise) when things aren't going well. (133) When this ratio is reversed to praising four or five times more than criticizing, things can go very well in the classroom. A teacher can maintain this praise/criticism ratio by saying penance after having criticized a student. Every time on verbally criticizing any student, the teacher must immediately make at least five different nice comments to five different students before again criticizing any other student. This penance technique helps to insure that praise is increased and spread among more students. Besides, no criticism takes place during the penance. The result is a more positive atmosphere in the classroom or the gymnasium. Actually teachers can criticize as much as they want as long as they keep the 5:1 praise/criticism ratio. A teacher will invariably criticize every now and then, but keeping to a 5:1 ratio, criticizing in an atmosphere of praise, will help achieve success. (29,133)

6. *Criticize softly and directly* to the individual(s) involved. Behavioral studies have demonstrated that loud reprimands may actually increase the inappropriate behaviors of some students while soft reprimands resulted in better control for many students. (164) Instead of yelling at someone across the gym, or a playing field, walk over to the individual, when possible, and speak softly. Someone having been yelled at is most apt to yell back. Yelling loudly is a common antecedent event which can quickly escalate into a shouting battle between a teacher and student(s). It's better to criticize softly and praise loudly.

The suggestions made thus far, about enhancing a teacher's social consequences so that they can function as possible social reinforcements for students, have only dealt with a teacher's verbal praises. Nonverbal social consequences such as a smile, a pat on the back, a nod of the head, etc. are also social consequences which can also function as social reinforcements. (107) These nonverbal social consequences invariably accompany verbal praises and should, of course, be used as much as possible. The wealth of behavior modification research in the schools has concerned primarily the effects a teacher's verbal praises can have on students' behaviors. It is much easier to keep track of verbal praises than nonverbal social consequences. Because it's easier to count verbal praises than nonverbal consequences and because so many behavioral studies have shown how very effective verbal praise is in improving behaviors, the behavior modification approach advocates that teachers try to maximize the extent to which they verbally praise their students.

Physical education teachers should be forewarned. Once a teacher begins to change his or her own classroom behaviors (dispensing more praise than usual), students will become aware of it and a short period of stress and storm may arise as everyone involved gets used to the teacher's new behavior patterns. If students show some concern for what's happening, and/or if a teacher becomes somewhat embarrassed or self-conscious about what is going on, it is a very good sign. It means that the teacher is actually making changes in the teaching procedures and that something is happening. Keep it up. It should lead to improvements in the students' performance.

It's more difficult to change some teachers' behaviors than others. As one study showed, keeping a chart of one's praises to students was not effective in increasing the praising behavior of every teacher. (234) When the teachers then had tones piped intermittantly into their classrooms over an intercom and were to praise a student whenever they heard a tone, more teachers increased their praising behavior. There are other procedures for changing a teacher's behaviors when a teacher may not be able to do it too well alone. As a matter of fact, a great deal of recent behavioral work has been concerned with how best to teach teachers and others to change their interactions with students and others they interact with during their everyday lives. A recent book on training individuals in the use of behavior modification procedures should be very valuable to physical education teachers and/or college professors of physical education. It has a number of articles on teaching others how to use behavior modification procedures in the school, the home, and other settings. (251) A recent article has a very useful summary of studies concerned with teaching others how to use behavior modification procedures, and it offers very specific guidelines on how best to do this. (125) It should be particularly worthwhile for anyone involved in either pre-service or in-service training of physical education teachers.

The "Bug-in-the-Ear" as a Training Device

A problem in helping teachers change their behaviors in the classroom is how to give them immediate feedback about what they are doing. If a supervising teacher or someone else does this as a teacher is teaching, it can interfere with what the teacher is doing. If feedback is given after a lesson, it is not of any use to the teacher until some future time, and even so, it may not be of any practical use at all because a similar situation where the advice may be put to work may not happen to the teacher for some days, weeks, or even months. This problem exists whether feedback is given orally or in the form of TV feedback of a teacher's performance. But how can someone give a teacher immediate feedback to a student's performance that doesn't interfere with what is going on and that can be immediately used by a teacher to improve teaching? One very effective way of doing this by having a teacher wear a "bug-in-the-ear."

The bug-in-the-ear is a physical device which has been rather extensively used to improve teachers' behaviors, and which has also been found to be useful in improving students' behaviors. It has also been very useful as a training device in directly improving the behavior of children and husbands and wives at home. It can be extremely useful in physical education settings, both in the training of teachers and/or coaches and their students and/or athletes. The bug-in-the-ear is a radio-controlled receiver which fits into the ear like a hearing aid. Such a device can be obtained commercially or handmade in various ways. (214) Nowadays many individuals own Citizen Band radios, and they can easily be adapted to be used with a bug-in-the-ear. In using a bug-in-the-ear a teacher or coach could just talk into a microphone, and the student and/or athlete wearing the bug-in-the-ear would hear what was being said, regardless of what was happening all around him or her and regardless of how noisy it is. This radio-controlled device allows a teacher to give immediate individualized verbal attention to a student without disrupting the student's activity or of those around the student. A teacher could continually guide and shape a student's responses even at long distance with this device. With variations and adaptions the bug-in-the-ear can be used with a number of individuals at the same time, as in teaching or coaching a number of individuals on a team simultaneously. The bug-in-the-ear promises to be a most important innovation in physical education for giving students the kind of immediate feedback which will positively benefit them in improving upon their physical fitness and athletic skills.

ACTIVITY REINFORCEMENT PROCEDURES

Most students' behaviors will improve when their teacher systematically increases just his or her social consequences. For those that don't, other kinds of consequences may have to be used in addition to verbal praises. (22) Conceivably any kind of an event can be used by a teacher as a consequence for a student's behavior. Physical educators and coaches have always used a wide variety of incentives or awards for students and/or athletes. Coaching journals are full of articles describing ways to motivate athletes, from giving them decals for their helmets in football (218), or placing stars on a bulletin board in baseball (91), to giving them points or tokens for their performances which they can then exchange for decals (34), ice cream (168), or other kinds of awards, even varsity letters. (148) These kinds of consequences may be quite effective in many cases, whereas in other cases they may not work at all. Regardless of whether they work or not, the teacher or coach who uses them is trying to increase or improve behaviors by manipulating consequences.

Giving objects of various kinds for performance can increase desirable behaviors; if so, the objects are functioning as reinforcements. Other kinds of consequences can also be effective. Two very important kinds of consequences which have been extensively studied in educational settings are activity and token reinforcements. The teacher who lets Juan work on the trampoline if he comes to the gym on time, who lets Mary work on the uneven bars if she helps other students rope climb, and who lets Larry help with clean-up if he does his headstand exercises correctly, is a teacher who is letting these students do something they really like to do if they first do something they might not like doing very much. Teachers and parents frequently use these kinds of consequences without realizing they may be using a reinforcement procedure. "Brush your teeth, and then you can go out and play," or "Do your homework, and then you can watch TV," are examples of using activity consequences. Behavioral studies have shown that a disliked behavior can be increased in frequency if the person is allowed to do some activity he or she really likes to do immediately after. In other words, following a low preference behavior by a high preference behavior often leads to an increase in frequency of the low preference behavior. In this situation, a person's behavior functions as a reinforcement for another one of his or her behaviors; the individual is actually reinforcing himself or herself. Self-reinforcement has very important implications for adults and others who are concerned about keeping physically fit. Using activity consequences for exercising or dieting can function as reinforcements and can help one keep physically fit. Examples of how adults have used activity reinforcements as consequences for their exercising will be discussed later.

An activity reinforcement is defined as *any activity (behavior) an individual engages in following his or her own behavior which increases the occurrence of the behavior in the future.* Using activity reinforcements to change and improve behaviors is sometimes referred to as using the "Premack Principle," "Contingency Contracting," or "Grandma's Rule." Each of these terms are synonymous, and refer to the fact that many people will increase doing something they don't like to do in order to do something they like to do.

The activity an individual engages in following his performing a low preference behavior can take place at school, at home, or any other place. (180) Some examples of using activity reinforcements in physical education settings are: additional recreation time for getting a new member to come to a recreation center (173), being taken out to dinner for keeping the weightroom clean (49), and missing practice for improving one's pole vaulting. (21) Finding out what activities students like can be determined by watching what they do in their free time, asking them directly, or finding lists of possible activities from behavior modification guides. A recent book lists many such activities. It also lists well over 200 different verbal praise words and sentences which teachers may find useful for varying the praises they give to their students. (132:178–80) Another source lists 65 verbal praise statements. (114)

Using activities as consequences for a student's behaviors amounts to making a verbal contract. If a student does something for the teacher, then the teacher will do something in return. Such contracts, which can also be put in written form, are especially useful in the upper grades. A recent book gives details on how to construct and use such written contracts. (53) For very young children, or some students in adaptive education classes, very effective picture contracts (cartoons), which don't require any reading on the part of the student, will be found to be very useful. (115) When using activity reinforcements (and token reinforcement procedures also), it is important that students be actively involved in selecting the particular consequences and in defining the behavior that has to precede the desired activity. When students decide upon these things, they perform much better than when the teacher unilaterally imposes his or her own expectations on them. (127) Activity reinforcement procedures can be used with single individuals or with a whole class. A very useful summary of group contingency procedures in educational settings can be consulted for more detailed information. (86)

TOKEN REINFORCEMENT PROCEDURES

In most school situations students don't usually have an immediate opportunity to engage in activity consequences or to be given some sort of material consequence such as awards, decals, etc., for successfully exhibiting some behavior. These consequences may be given to them at the end of a class period, later on during the day or week, or at home or some other place. In some instances the consequences may have to take place some time in the future, and it may be one or more weeks, or even many months before a student receives a consequence he or she has been working for. To bridge the time gap between exhibiting appropriate physical education and/or athletic behaviors and receiving the desired consequences teachers and/or coaches may give students points or tokens. Once a certain number of these tokens are accumulated, then the students would be able to turn them in for material objects or activities for which they are working. Receiving money for working is an example of using tokens, for the money can be turned in for various goods or activities. We live in a token economy.

It is easy to find examples of token systems in physical education publications. There are general discussions about using them (6), discussions about using them for grading systems (63,147), in football (34), or cross-country training (148,168), to mention but a few. Although such point or token systems may be quite widely used by both teachers and coaches, very few of them are using the point or token systems as effectively as they can. One apparent reason for this is that they are unaware of the hundreds of published behavior modification studies on using token reinforcement procedures in school and other settings. The physical education articles on token systems show many deficiencies in the various applications of the token systems they describe. The situation may have been such that a student can only win once, even though he or she has accumulated a number of points for good behavior (148), or such that they can't individualize a student's program, or use shaping procedures with him or her, or such that students may not obtain the consequences they have worked for. Students may even have to do tedious work unnecessarily, such as jogging, in order to obtain consequences they had already earned. (168) Physical education teachers and coaches should be cautioned against using token reinforcement procedures, especially with a whole group of students or athletes, unless they are very well versed in the ABC's of the behavioral approach. Many things can go wrong in using a token economy. For example, daily records of earnings and spending may not be kept and inflations and/or depressions can occur, students may steal tokens, students may earn too many tokens and they may not want to work anymore, students may lose all of their tokens and go bankrupt, they may be overtrained with a token system and become too dependent on it, they may not be able to turn their tokens in soon enough for them to be effective, or they may not have enough varied activities or material goods they can turn their tokens in for. A real-life example illustrates what can go wrong. (116)

Teachers should become familiar with the published behavior modification studies of token reinforcement programs that bear directly on their area of interest, and acquire a basic knowledge of the behavioral approach, especially pinpointing, counting, recording, charting, and evaluating what is happening, before ever attempting to conduct a large scale token reinforcement program.

Much information is available to guide one in using token reinforcement procedures. An excellent article reviews token reinforcement systems in the schools (163), and a book discusses the use of token reinforcement procedures in school settings in great detail. (239) A similar book should be most useful for teachers in adaptive physical education settings, or for any teacher who has to deal with similar problems. It offers very concrete and specific suggestions. (156) A recent article provides teachers with a systematic overview of common problems in running a token economy. (55) It describes the problems, suggests how to remedy them, and most important, explains how to structure the situation so that they don't occur. It is required reading for anyone contemplating using an elaborate token system with a group of students or athletes. In addition to these potential technical problems, one must be aware that the administrators and the parents may have reservations or outright hostility toward such procedures. One should be prepared to deal with these concerns before beginning any such program.

A frequently voiced criticism of the token reinforcement procedure is that it constitutes bribing. This criticism is a common misconception about using tokens. Knowing how to respond to such a criticism can facilitate using such procedures with one's students. Using tokens or points to teach children to read, write, or perform well in physical education is not bribing. A definition of bribing is *giving money and/or favors to someone doing something illegal or immoral*. It certainly isn't illegal or immoral for children or adults to learn to read or write or perform well in physical education, and many other activities. Another common concern is that students always have to be given tokens to do their schoolwork. Correct usage of token reinforcement procedures requires students to be gradually weaned from them. Generally verbal praise would always be used with the tokens so that when the tokens are finally taken away, verbal praise alone would maintain the desired behavior.

A wide variety of criticisms and concerns about behavior

modification in general, and token reinforcement procedures in particular, have been expressed from time to time. (249) Most of these concerns reflect a lack of information about the nature of behavior modification and the correct use of the various behavioral procedures, including token economies. Two very good discussions of these common concerns are readily available and should be read and studied by anyone contemplating the use of token reinforcement procedures in school settings. (162,165) Once one becomes fully acquainted with the substance of these articles, one will be better able to understand and answer the more common kinds of questions which are asked about behavior modification procedures in general and about particular token reinforcement techniques.

Before implementing a token reinforcement program, especially if it is with a whole group of students or athletes, one should become thoroughly acquainted with the more relevant references mentioned above. If possible, one should also observe someone who is successfully using a token reinforcement program in a school or physical education setting, and talk to them about the intricacies of using tokens with students. Token reinforcement procedures were used in the previously mentioned studies dealing with weightlifting (49), pole vaulting (21), walking (190,197), posture (57), competition among handicapped children (110), and exercising. (101) Cooper's aerobic training program (40) is structured so that points are obtained for following the program. The points alone, as consequences, may be effective for many individuals to persist in the program. Keeping a chart of the points obtained may make the point system more effective. One might even use them as tokens to be turned in for various activities or other consequences. Cooper even suggested to one individual who had trouble getting adolescents to stick to the aerobic program that he might give them various kinds of patches for the points they earned. (40:164) He was suggesting a simple token system. Because his system involves shaping and a point system which had been very carefully and scientifically determined, his system can be very easily incorporated into a token reinforcement program. Combined with a token reinforcement program it promises to be a very important and effective way of improving the physical fitness of literally many, many thousands of young students and adults of all ages. The previously mentioned study of how a young woman earned quarters for jogging according to the criteria of Cooper's program illustrates how a token program can be very successfully combined with his program to improve someone's physical well-being substantially. (101)

PUNISHMENT PROCEDURES

When students engage in behaviors which are dangerous in any way, which seriously interfere with their own learning or that of others, or which for other reasons may be deemed by a teacher or others to be maladaptive, teachers will want to decrease these kinds of behaviors very quickly. Because numerous studies have demonstrated that merely ignoring behaviors often won't make them go away (130,183), it is necessary to do something to stop or decrease the behaviors quickly. An excellent discussion of the nature of punishment that will help to dispel many common misconceptions can be found in a very informative book of use to teachers, coaches, and parents. (12)

Unfortunately when many individuals try to punish others for their inappropriate behaviors, they often do so in a vindictive and harsh manner. Students may be made to do something they don't like to do, they may be kept after school, or they may even be suspended from school or an athletic team. If a student swears at a teacher, it would not be uncommon for the teacher to hold a grudge against the student. As a result of this grudge, the teacher won't interact with the student in the future as positively as in the immediate past, and the effect of this will be that the student will be ignored by the teacher sometimes when he or she is behaving appropriately. Holding a grudge has the effect of reducing positive social interaction between individuals. Ignoring the appropriate behaviors of students who have misbehaved is a very common error of both teachers and parents. It is crucial not to be vindictive, not to hold grudges against students, not to use excessively harsh punishments, and not to ignore the appropriate behaviors of students if one wants to bring inappropriate behaviors under control. The teacher should always catch the student being good and interact positively, whether or not the student has behaved inappropriately in the immediate past. Catching students only when they are being bad does nothing to increase more appropriate behaviors. If students are taught to exhibit appropriate behaviors that are incompatible with their inappropriate behaviors, they would be sure to be behaving appropriately since they can't be doing two things at the same time. A rule in using the behavior modification approach is to always catch students being good. Try to catch them being good 100 percent of the time. When students behave in a manner which warrants doing something to decrease that particular behavior quickly, an appropriate punishment procedure can be used. At the same time the teacher should continue to catch the student being good.

Any consequence, as long as it decreases the frequency of a behavior in the future, can function as a punishment. Counting and/or charting one's own behavior may result in a decrease in the behavior. (23) Temporarily removing a student from a situation for behaving inappropriately (time-out) may also decrease the frequency of certain behaviors. (237) The time-out procedure can be very effective if used correctly (14); it can also be used with a whole group of students, even on a moving school bus. (183) A very flexible and effective punishment procedure which can be used with either individuals or a whole group of students involves a fining procedure, and is called "response cost." (103) In response cost, individuals lose points or tokens or privileges when they exhibit an inappropriate behavior. Examples of the use of response cost procedures with single individuals can be found in a variety of places. (47,68,80,103) The previously mentioned study of pole vaulting used a response cost procedure with each athlete. (21) Using response cost procedures with whole groups or classes of students has also been extensively studied. (86) The studies where all of the children lost recreation time for rule infractions (173), or where a weight room would be closed for everyone if a certain number of weights were left on the floor (49), are examples of group response cost procedures. In an interesting study done with a number of high school gym classes, the total number of students coming to class on time increased when a group response cost procedure was used. Having the whole class repeat some exercises many times more than usual if any student was late led immediately to almost perfect punctuality for each of five different classes. (68:134–37)

It should be mentioned that although this particular punishment technique worked, this kind of a group procedure, where all suffer for the mistakes of others, can produce a number of unwanted and serious side effects. Students may become very hostile toward the late arriving students, and this might adversely affect their social interactions. It can also affect the students interactions with their physical education teacher, who may be considered to be unfair. Any kind of group punishment technique can backfire or produce serious unwanted side effects unless used carefully. This is one reason to learn carefully the fundamentals of the behavioral approach before attempting to use it, and why one should carefully read and study the published works of others who have previously used such procedures successfully. Doing this will help to prevent failures. A recent article reviewing the use of group procedures in the schools (86), among others, would need to be consulted before attempting to use a procedure such as that mentioned above.

To be effective, punishment procedures should be applied consistently (173), and the consequences should occur immediately after a student exhibits the behavior, instead of a few hours, days, or weeks later. (49) Several sources very useful to teachers and coaches provide step-by-step models of various punishment and reinforcement procedures audiovisually. (26,29) An important guideline in using behavior modification procedures of any kind is that one should be thoroughly versed in the behavior modification approach and the particular procedures being used. Regardless of what one may be trying to accomplish, by first reading others' research, and then pinpointing, counting, charting, changing environments, and continually monitoring and evaluating what is happening—all of this will help students improve their behaviors.

KEEPING PHYSICALLY FIT BY USING
SELF-MODIFICATION PROCEDURES

Developing life-long physical fitness skills is the most important goal of any physical education curriculum. Most individuals, unfortunately, haven't developed such skills, and as a result most adults aren't as physically fit, active, or healthy as they should be. (93) A proper diet and regular exercise may be very important for everyone, but most people find it difficult to do either and consequently develop cardiovascular and other kinds of health problems. Since the problem is so pervasive, there is a growing national concern for keeping physically fit.

It has been suggested that a very important emerging role for the physical educator could be that of an exercise specialist on health teams. In order to function in this capacity such specialists would have to be broadly trained in physical education and human behavior, as well as be skilled in techniques for getting individuals to change and modify their lifestyles so that they will exercise properly. (62) Determining and prescribing what kinds of exercises a particular individual should do, along with their intensity, frequency, and duration, is relatively easy for the physical educator. But getting individuals to do them on their own, in a self-motivated and conscientious manner, can be very difficult. Doing this often involves changing and modifying a lifestyle. The behavior modification approach can make substantial contributions not only in helping to solve these problems, but in teaching the young life-long physical fitness habits and skills.

Getting young children, young adults, or adults to exercise on their own amounts to getting them to improve and maintain their own behaviors by themselves. In effect they are being asked to use self-modification procedures. Teaching individuals how to improve their own behaviors by using self-modification procedures is a very important and extensive area of applied behavior modification research. Research on helping physically unfit adults to exercise correctly and frequently shouldn't be overlooked by the physical educators. Being involved actively in changing and improving one's own behavior is a very important element of the behavior modification approach. In fact, all of the behavior modification procedures which have been discussed in this guide may be used as techniques for teaching individuals how to change and improve their own behaviors. Furthermore, an individual could apply these procedures to his own behavior directly. Under these circumstances behavior modification procedures become self-improvement procedures. This can work for nervous habits of various kinds, such as fingernail biting or scratching. It can also work for such things as talking-out in school (23), or swimming. (149) Benjamin Franklin used, for his day, rather sophisticated self-modification procedures to help him improve such virtues as temperance, frugality, and moderation. (112) He kept a daily table of the number of errors he made in exhibiting each of 13 different virtues. At the end of each day, he consulted the table to determine virtues he was not practicing well enough, and this feedback helped him to identify the virtues that required more effort. Each day he tried to keep the table for that day completely free of tallies, for each tally would indicate he had erred on one of the virtues. He found this procedure to be quite successful for him. We have come a long way since the days of Ben Franklin, and some current research has been devoted to determining the most optimal ways to use self-modification procedures. (105,136) Quite a few books have also been written on the topic. (151,231,241) One of these books devotes an entire chapter to the use of such procedures for developing one's sports behaviors (246), although the discussion is very general.

These behavior modification self-improvement books are quite suitable for classes in high school and college and for use with most adults. They discuss the technicalities and practicalities of using the behavior modification approach for self-modification. Each of them goes through the steps discussed thus far in this guide, pinpointing behaviors to be improved, counting and charting them, changing something in order to improve the behavior (antecedents and/or consequences), and then, if one didn't succeed, trying again.

To illustrate how the behavior modification approach can be successfully used to help adults improve their present level of exercising, several examples of self-modification of exercising will be briefly discussed. These projects, with one exception, were done by individuals ranging in age from the early 20's to mid-40's. Each of them learned how to apply the behavior modification approach to their exercising behaviors while enrolled in a graduate course on behavior modification. Although these particular individuals learned these skills taking a college graduate level course, the skills can be taught in any setting, in or out of school, and to individuals of any age, or educational backgrounds. Table 6 shows the exercising behaviors each of them wanted to improve, the general procedure they used, and the results they obtained.

It should be mentioned that the individuals whose self-modification projects are represented in Table 6 had tried unsuccessfully to improve their exercising on their own before they began to use a self-modification procedure. In this respect they are representative of the millions of individuals who know that they should be doing something positive to keep physically fit, but don't actually do so. The success each of these individuals experienced in a very short period of time shows how powerful and effective the behavior modification approach is in helping people to keep physically fit.

Three of these self-modification projects involved the use of activity reinforcements. One woman wanted to increase the amount of time she spent practicing ballet at home. (28) During 7 days of baseline observations she averaged around 12 minutes of practice a day, 20 minutes being the most she ever practiced. She enjoyed leisure-time reading of various sorts, and so she decided that she would give herself 1 minute of reading time for every minute she practiced her ballet beyond 20 minutes a day. Thus the only way she could engage in any leisure-time reading was to practice her ballet more than 20 minutes a day. On the first day she practiced 30 minutes, and on the second she practiced 75 minutes. During the 5-week period that she continued to keep a chart of her ballet practice she averaged around 60 minutes practice a day, a 400 percent increase over her average practice time during the baseline period. Her increased practice resulted in several other consequences, both of which helped her to continue practicing and to

TABLE 6—SOME EXAMPLES OF HOW ADULTS HAVE USED THE BEHAVIOR MODIFICATION APPROACH TO IMPROVE EXERCISING AND SPORTS BEHAVIORS

Behavior	Self-Modification Procedure	Results
ballet practice at home	activity reinforcement (leisure-time reading)	increase from 12 to 60 minutes/day
Yoga exercises	activity reinforcement (newspaper reading)	increase from 0 to 20 minutes/day
laps swum	activity reinforcement (television watching)	increase from 20 to 40 laps/day
holes of golf	token reinforcement (money, skip mowing the lawn, ride to pro lessons)	increase from 4 to 12 holes/day
six different exercises	token reinforcement (money for sailing trip)	increase from 4 to 14 push-ups and 9 to 30 other exercises/day
three different exercises	token reinforcement (money for paperback books)	increase from 65 to 102 exercises/day
walking	response-cost punishment (donate $5 to charity for walking fewer than 20 blocks)	increase from 4 to 28 blocks/day

improve her ballet skills. During the first two days of her self-improvement program her ballet teacher praised her very warmly for her improved performance in class. As she practiced more and more, she noticed a visible change in her musculature and in the flexibility of her joints and limbs. Both of these consequences which were produced by increased practice were considered by her to be very important in helping her to continue in her ballet practice at home.

Another woman used an activity reinforcement to help her do her Yoga exercises. (35) She had bought a popular book on how to get slimmer by doing Yoga exercises, but although she had enjoyed reading the book, she rarely practiced the exercises and might go as long as a month or so without ever doing any Yoga exercises. Obviously, reading the book was not enough to get her to do the exercises. Assuming that her experience is somewhat representative of the effects such self-help books have, her project shows how useful the behavior modification approach can be in taking a book describing physical exercises, and implementing it to get actual physical exercising. During a 7-day baseline period she never practiced her Yoga exercises. She decided to make newspaper reading dependent upon doing Yoga exercises, and she further decided that she would give herself 2 minutes of newspaper reading for each minute of Yoga exercising she did. On the first day she began her project she practiced her Yoga for 12 minutes, and for the next 8-day period she was doing it an average of 20 minutes a day. One effect of her success in exercising regularly was that she felt much better after exercising, and that she even looked forward to her exercise sessions each day (something she had never done before).

An activity reinforcement was also used by a man who wanted to increase the number of laps he swam each day in an Olympic-sized pool. (72) During 5 days of baseline recording he swam 20 laps a day. He decided to make his TV watching dependent upon the number of laps he swam, and he gave himself 2 minutes of TV watching for each lap over 20 that he swam each day. On the first day of his self-modification program he swam 35 laps, an increase of 15 over his baseline efforts. During the next week and a half he averaged around 40 laps a day, a 100 percent increase over his baseline performance. On several days he swam 60 laps, more than he had ever swum in his lifetime.

Three of the projects summarized in Table 6 involved the use of a token reinforcement procedure. In one of these an elementary school principal taught his son how to use a self-improvement procedure to increase the number of holes of golf he played each day. (51) He wanted his son to play golf for his own sake and also he wanted him to try out for the high school golf team. For 5 days, each day he casually asked his son how many holes of golf he played that day at a nearby golf course. He obtained his baseline data in this fashion, and it showed that his son averaged 4 holes of golf a day. It varied from a high of 9 holes per day to 0 holes on 2 days when he didn't play at all. At this point the boy's father asked his son to keep a record of the holes of golf he played each day, and told him that he would chart the record for him each day. For the next 5 days his son played every day and averaged 6 holes per day. Then he instituted a token program with his son for the next 5 days. The son agreed that he would receive a token for each hole of golf he played each day. The tokens he would earn by playing golf were exchangable for a number of mutually agreed upon things. Each token could be turned in for 15¢, 45 tokens could be turned in for the privilege of not cutting the lawn (one of his weekly chores), 15 tokens could be turned in for the privilege of not cutting any of three different sections of the lawn, some tokens could be turned in for a basket of golf balls at a driving range, or some tokens could be turned in for a ride to the golf pro for golf lessons. During the first day of the token procedure he shot 17 holes of golf, and averaged 12 holes per day during the 5 days of the token program.

One man used a token system to increase his frequency of doing six different exercises, push-ups, sit-ups, squat thrusts, leg lowering, trunk rolls, and jumping jacks. (48) During 7 days of baseline counting he averaged only 4 push-ups per day, and around 9 each of the other exercises. Then he began a three-phase token program in which he had to exceed his previous week's performance for each exercise in order to earn tokens (a shaping procedure). Each token was worth a certain amount of money. The tokens could be accumulated and exchanged for money to pay for a weekend sailing trip. During the last week of this program he was averaging 14 push-ups a day, and 30 each for each of the other exercises. He increased the time he was exercising from 15 minutes during baseline to 45 minutes during the end of his token program, an increase of 200 percent, and he increased the number of exercises he was doing by 300 percent. He mentioned that the three phase program allowed him to increase gradually without any undue discomfort or inconvenience. Gradual increases in physical activity is desirable. It is a basic component of Cooper's aerobic training program (40), and it facilitated exercising in this case, although the individual was not using Cooper's program. Even so, this project illustrates how one can receive tokens for a number of different exercises, something which is built into Cooper's program.

A woman also used a token procedure to increase her exercising.

(203) She wanted to increase how often she did sit-ups, swivel toe-touches, and leg-raises. Her goal was to do at least 100 of them in any combination each day. During the 4 days of charting her baseline, the number of her exercises done increased from 65 to 88 per day. She mentioned that just counting and charting the exercising made her very much aware of what she was doing each day, and that this helped her improve her exercising. This is an example of charting functioning as a reinforcement. During the next 5 days she decided to give herself 1¢ for each exercise she did. The money she paid herself for exercising would be used to get a number of paperback books she very much wanted. During these 5 days she averaged around 102 exercises a day.

The last example in Table 6 shows how a woman used a punishment procedure to help her increase the amount of walking she does each day. (224) She had been used to getting from place to place by using public transportation—subways, buses, and taxis. When she took 5 days of baseline recording on her walking she found that she only walked around 4 blocks a day. She set a goal of at least 20 blocks a day (around 1 mile) and decided to use a response cost procedure (103) to increase her walking. If she didn't walk at least 20 blocks a day, then she would "punish" herself by writing out a check for $5 to some charity. At the time she was using this procedure she was unemployed and spending money on charity would have been a burden for her. The first day she implemented this response cost punishment procedure she walked 26 blocks. For the next 10 days that she recorded her walking under the punishment contingency, she walked between 20 to 37 blocks a day, averaging 28 blocks per day, an increase of 600 percent over her baseline walking performance. Because she had never walked less than the minimum number of blocks she set for herself, she never had to pay any fine.

As each of the self-modification projects shows, adults can easily learn how to apply behavior modification procedures to improve their physical fitness. The case of the elementary school principal shows how a father who learned about this approach helped one of his children to exercise more frequently and to become more proficient in a sports activity. These are but a few examples of how adults throughout the country are learning to use the behavior modification approach to improve their physical fitness. The success which was obtained in teaching these adults how to use self-modification procedures to improve their exercising can be repeated by physical educators who master the fundamentals of the behavior modification approach and apply it in their own settings. Once physical educators learn the ABC's of the behavior modification approach, it can become for them a very important tool in helping them to better teach individuals of any age to improve their physical fitness.

THE FUTURE OF THE BEHAVIOR MODIFICATION APPROACH IN PHYSICAL EDUCATION

On the basis of the discussion in this report on the applications of behavior modification procedures for helpings students, athletes, and adults improve their physical fitness, athletic, and/or social behaviors, one can only conclude that the behavior modification approach is highly useful in helping to implement physical education curriculums into practice. There are other areas within physical education, teaching health education, teaching automobile driving skills, supervising individuals in recreational or leisure-time activities, and managing athletic and recreational activities in camping facilities, where the behavior modification approach can also be quite helpful. These areas have also been extensively studied by behavior modification researchers. A brief discussion of some of the behavioral research in these areas will show that the future of the behavior modification approach in physical education goes far beyond what many would expect.

Supervising and training individuals in recreational and leisure-time activities and sports is an area which should expand rapidly in the near future as the amount of time available for leisure has been increasing over the years. Applications of the behavior modification approach in this area can be found in studies of children of various ages (172,173), of retarded individuals (181,242), and of geriatric adults. (145) Many times physical educators may function in managerial roles where they have to supervise others who provide recreational services directly. Behavioral procedures can be of use to the manager as well. (125) For example, behavioral procedures have been shown to be very effective in getting adolescent physical education aides to adequately perform such roles as outdoor recreation or tournament supervisors. (172) Although physical educators who work in outdoor camping situations have many of the same problems as those working indoors, there are some that are peculiar to the camping situations. A summary of behavior modification in camp settings can be found in a book which is devoted entirely to using the behavior modification approach in camping. (182)

Although relatively little behavior modification research has been directly done on teaching automobile driving skills, those physical educators who are involved in driver training can quite easily make use of basic behavioral principles and procedures to help them teach safe driving habits. Behavior modification procedures have been developed for helping individuals to reduce the frequency of accidents (109), even those which are alcohol-related. (126) One interesting study demonstrated how to use behavioral procedures to teach young children auto-pedestrian safety behaviors. (94)

The general consensus among physical educators is that helping students with personal health problems should be an integral part of any physical education curriculum. (169) Teaching individuals proper health practices and helping them correct improper health-related behaviors are very important. This area has been quite thoroughly investigated and behavioral procedures have been used to improve a wide variety of common health problems. (99) Drug addiction, alcoholism, smoking, and overeating leading to obesity have been quite thoroughly studied, and a number of different remedial and preventative procedures have been developed to deal with these problems. A recent behavioral journal, *Addictive Behaviors,* is entirely devoted to publishing behavioral articles on dealing with drug addiction, alcoholism, smoking, and obesity—a sign that the amount of work being done in these areas is very substantial. Two books have chapters reviewing recent behavioral work done on the addictions (44,166), and their usefulness to physical educators should be immediately apparent. Several reviews of behavior modofication research on weight reduction are quite instructive. (221,222) One of them traces the history of both medical and behavioral research on weight reduction (221) concluding that behavior modification procedures have been demonstrated to be the most effective techniques yet developed to teach overweight individuals to change their eating habits so as to lose substantial amounts of weight, and most important, keep from regaining the lost weight. An excellent guide for using behavior modification procedures in weight reduction programs discusses many practical details of the procedures. (220)

The application of behavioral procedures to personal health problems at this stage of development of the behavior modification approach has been so successful that one can be very optimistic about what this approach will offer in the very near future. This optimism has been reflected in an article which recently appeared in one of the most important medical journals in the world, the *New England Journal of Medicine*. The article is on the role of behavior modification in preventive medicine. The authors of the article make a very strong statement about the future utility of the behavior modification approach:

> Although much work remains to be done, we believe that the successful application of behavioral principles to problems in preventive medicine may prove to be as important a contribution to medical practice as the development of effective antibacterial agents was in the first half of the century. (176:1277)

One important goal of physical education is teaching individuals lifelong sound health practices. Physical educators who learn about and use the behavior modification approach with their students and/or athletes, will find that it can help them in meeting this and other important physical education goals.

References

SELECTED RESEARCH REFERENCES

1. Allen, G. "Football Like Life Is a Game of Basics." *The Athletic Journal* 53:22, 104; April 1973.
2. Allen, K. E. "What Teachers of Young Exceptional Children Can Do." *Teaching Exceptional Children* 2:119–27; 1972.
3. American Psychiatric Association. *Behavior Therapy in Psychiatry.* Wash., D. C.: the Association, 1973. 75 pp.
4. Anderson, W. G. "Descriptive-Analytic Research on Teaching." *Quest* 15:1–8; 1971.
5. Ayllon, T., and Azrin, N. *The Token Economy: A Motivational System for Therapy and Rehabilitation.* New York: Appleton-Century-Crofts, 1968. 288 pp.
6. Azrin, N., and others. "Behavioral Engineering: Postural Control by a Portable Operant Apparatus." *Journal of Applied Behavior Analysis* 1:99–108; 1968.
7. Baer, D. M.; Wolf, M.; and Risley, T. R. "Some Current Dimensions of Applied Behavior Analysis." *Journal of Applied Behavior Analysis* 1:91–97; 1968.
8. Bailey, J. S.; Wolf, M.; and Phillips, E. L. "Home-Based Reinforcement and the Modification of Pre-Delinquent Classroom Behavior." *Journal of Applied Behavior Analysis* 3:223–33; 1970.
9. Baker, J. G., and Whitehead, G. "A Portable Apparatus for Rating Behavior in Free-Operant Situations." *Journal of Applied Behavior Analysis* 5:191–92; 1972.
10. Bandura, A. *Principles of Behavior Modification.* New York: Holt, Rinehart and Winston, 1969. 677 pp.
11. Barlow, D. H.; Reynolds, E. J.; and Agras, W. S. "Gender Identity Change in a Transsexual." *Archives of General Psychiatry* 28:569–601; 1973.
12. Becker, W. C. *Parents Are Teachers.* Champaign, Ill.: Research Press, 1971. 200 pp.

13.   _____; Engelmann, S.; and Thomas, D. R. *Teaching 2: Cognitive Learning and Instruction.* Chicago: Science Research Associates, 1975. 263 pp.

14.   Benoit, R. B., and Mayer, C. R. "Timeout: Guidelines for its Selection and Use." *Personnel and Guidance Journal* 53:501–506; 1975.

15.   Berger, E. A. "Effects of Knowledge of Isometric Strength During Performance on Recorded Strength." *Research Quarterly* 38:507; 1967.

16.   Berman, M. L. "Instructions and Behavior Change: A Taxonomy." *Exceptional Children* 39:644–50; 1973.

17.   Bijou, S. W. "What Psychology Has to Offer Education—Now!" *Journal of Applied Behavior Analysis* 3:65–71; 1970.

18.   Bollenbacher, D. "Motivation Is the Key." *Coaching Clinic* 12: 8–9; August 1974.

19.   Bookhout, E. C. "Teaching Behavior in Relation to the Social-Emotional Climate of Physical Education Classes." *Research Quarterly* 38:336–47; 1967.

20.   Brault, D., and others. "Essentials of a Quality Elementary School Physical Education Program: A Position Paper." *Journal of Health, Physical Education, and Recreation* 42:42–46; April 1971.

21.   Brock, S.; Brock, D.; and Willis, J. "The Effect of Tangible and Token Rewards on the Pole Vaulting Behavior of High School Students." *School Applications of Learning Theory* 4 (No. 3):32–37; 1972.

22.   Broden, M., and others. "Effects of Teacher Attention and a Token Reinforcement System in a Junior High School Special Education Class." *Exceptional Children* 36:341–49; 1970.

23.   _____; Hall, R. V.; and Mitts, V. "The Effects of Self-Recording on the Classroom Behavior of Two Eighth-Grade Students." *Journal of Applied Behavior Analysis* 4:191–99; 1971.

24.   Brooks, B. D. "Contingency Management as a Means of Reducing School Truancy." *Education* 95:206–11; 1975.

25.   Brown, P. L., and Elliot, R. "Control of Aggression in a Nursery School Class." *Journal of Experimental Child Psychology* 2:103–07; 1965.

26.   _____, and Presbie, R. J. *Behavior Modification Skills.* Cambridge, Mass.: Research Media, 1974.

27.   _____. *Behavior Modification in Business, Industry, and Government.* New Paltz, N.Y.: Behavior Improvement Associates (P. O. Box 296), 1976. 70 pp.

28.   Brown-Goldpaugh, B. "Increasing the Time Spent in Ballet Practice at Home Using an Activity Reinforcement." Unpublished manuscript. New Paltz: State University of New York, Psychology Department, 1975.

29. Buckhalter, B. A.; Presbie, R. J.; and Brown, P. L. *Behavior Improvement Program*. Chicago: Science Research Associates, 1974.

30. Buell, J., and others. "Collateral Social Development Accompanying Reinforcement of Outdoor Play in a Preschool Child." *Journal of Applied Behavior Analysis* 1:167–74; 1968.

31. Bussard, D. "Get More Out of Your Basketball Statistics." *Coaching Clinic* 13:27–30; December 1975.

32. Butterfield, W. H. "Instrumentation in Behavior Therapy." *Behavior Modification Procedure: A Sourcebook*. (Edited by E. J. Thomas) Chicago: Aldine, 1974. pp. 267–311.

33. Carlson, J. D., and Mayer, G. R. "Fading: A Behavioral Procedure to Increase Independent Behaviors." *The School Counselor* 18:193–97; 1974.

34. Carlson, R. "Motivation: One Key to Successful Football Coaching." *Coaching Clinic* 10: 2–4; July 1972.

35. Carner, L. A. "Establishing a Program of Regular Physical Exercise Using Activity Reinforcement." Unpublished manuscript. New York: Pace University, Psychology Department, 1976.

36. Carnes, J. "Teaching the Hurdles." *The Athletic Journal* 53:56–57, 62; February 1973.

37. Caskey, S. R. "Effects of Motivation on Standing Broad Jump Performance of Children." *Research Quarterly* 39:54–59; 1968.

38. Cohen, S., and Hersh, R. "Behaviorism and Humanism: A Synthesis for Teacher Education." *The Journal of Teacher Education* 23:172–76; 1972.

39. Collins, D. "Motivating the Basketball Player." *Scholastic Coach* 42: 50, 52; October 1972.

40. Cooper, K. H. *The New Aerobics*. New York: M. Evans, 1970. 191 pp.

41. _____, and others. "An Aerobics Conditioning Program for the Fort Worth, Texas School District." *Research Quarterly* 46:345–50; 1975.

42. Copeland, R. W.; Brown, R. W.; and Hall, R. V. "The Effects of Principal-Implemented Techniques on the Behavior of Pupils." *Journal of Applied Behavior Analysis* 7:77–86; 1974.

43. Cotton, D. J., and Nixon, J. "A Comparison of Two Methods of Teaching the Tennis Serve." *Research Quarterly* 39:929–31; 1968.

44. Craighead, W. E.; Kazdin, A. E.; and Mahoney, M. J. *Behavior Modification: Principles, Issues and Applications*. Boston: Houghton Mifflin, 1976. 556 pp.

45. Csapo, M. "Pupils as Intervention Agents in Modifying Teacher Behavior." *School Applications of Learning Theory* 4 (No. 4):25–35; 1972.

46. Daniels, A. S., and Davis, E. A. *Adapted Physical Education*. New York: Harper and Row, 1975. 443 pp.

en110   PHYSICAL EDUCATION

47. Daniels, K., editor. *The Management of Childhood Behavior Problems in School and at Home.* Springfield, Ill.: C. C. Thomas, 1974. 456 pp.

48. D'Antuono, E. "Use of a Token Economy to Establish a Regular Habit of Exercise." Unpublished manuscript. New York: Pace University, Psychology Department, 1976.

49. Darden, E., and Madsen, C. H. "Behavior Modification for Weightlifting Room Problems." *College Student Journal* 6:95–99; 1972.

50. Dauer, V. P. *Dynamic Physical Education for Elementary School Children.* Minneapolis: Burgess, 1975. 574 pp.

51. Del Vecchio, J., Jr. "Increasing the Number of Holes of Golf Played Each Day with a Token Reinforcement Program." Unpublished manuscript. New Paltz, N. Y.: State University of New York, Psychology Department, 1976.

52. Deno, S. L., and Jenkins, J. R. "On the 'Behaviorality' of Behavioral Objectives." *Psychology in the Schools* 6:18–24, 1969.

53. DeRisi, W. J., and Butz, G. *Writing Behavioral Contracts: A Case Simulation Practice Manual.* Champaign, Ill.: Research Press, 1975. 87 pp.

54. Dissinger, J. K. "Accidents in Junior High School Physical Education Programs." *Research Quarterly* 37:495–504; 1966.

55. Drabman, R. S., and Tucker, R. D. "Why Classroom Token Economies Fail." *Journal of School Psychology* 12:178–88; 1974.

56. Dubois, P. E. "Personalize Your Weight Training Program." *The Physical Educator* 32:138–41; October 1975.

57. Duncan, P. K. "Modification of Walking Posture Using Basic Principles of Applied Behavior Analysis." *School Applications of Learning Theory* 6 (No. 2): 1–13; 1974.

58. Egner, A. N.; Burdett, C. S.; and Fox, W. L. *Observing and Measuring Class-Room Behaviors.* Austin, Texas: Austin Writers Group (P. O. Box 12642 Capitol Station), 1972. 71 pp.

59. Espenschade, A. S. *Physical Education in the Elementary Schools.* Wash., D. C.: National Education Association, 1963. 32 pp.

60. Evans, J. "Implications of Behavior Modification Techniques for the Physical Education Teacher." *The Physical Educator* 31:28–32, 1974.

61. Fallon, M. P., and Goetz, E. M. "The Creative Teacher: Effects of Descriptive Social Reinforcement upon the Drawing Behavior of Three Preschool Children." *School Applications of Learning Theory* 7 (No. 2):27–45; 1975.

62. Fardy, P. S., and Hellerstein, H. K. "An Emerging Role for the Physical Educator." *Quest* 24:80–84; 1975.

63. Fast, B. L. "Contracting." *Journal of Health, Physical Education, and Recreation* 42:31–32; September 1971.

64. Field, D. A. "Accountability for the Physical Educator." *Journal of Health, Physical Education, and Recreation* 44:37–38; February 1973.

65. Fischer, J., and Gochros, H. L. *Planned Behavior Change: Behavior Modification in Social Work.* New York: Free Press, 1975. 525 pp.

66. Fishman, S. E., and Anderson, W. G. "Developing a System for Describing Teaching." *Quest* 15:9–16; 1971.

67. Flanders, N. A. *Analyzing Teaching Behavior.* Reading, Mass.: Addison-Wesley, 1970. 448 pp.

68. Fox, R. G., and others. "A Computerized System for Selecting Responsive Teaching Studies, Catalogued Along Twenty-Eight Important Dimensions." *Behavior Analysis: Areas of Research and Application.* (Edited by E. Ramp, and G. Semb.) Englewood Cliffs, N. J.: Prentice-Hall, 1975. pp. 124–58.

69. Foxx, R. M., and Martin, P. L. "A Useful Portable Timer." *Journal of Applied Behavior Analysis* 4:60; 1971.

70. Fueyo, V.; Suadargas, R. A.; and Bushell, D., Jr. "Two Types of Feedback in Teaching Swimming Skills to Handicapped Children." *Perceptual and Motor Skills* 40:963–66; 1975.

71. Gelfand, D. M.; Gelfand, S.; and Dobson, W. R. "Unprogrammed reinforcement of patients' behavior in a mental hospital." *Behavior Research and Therapy* 5:201–207; 1967.

72. Glassman, A. "Increasing Swimming with a Television Watching Reinforcement." Unpublished manuscript. New Paltz, N. Y.: State University of New York, Psychology Department, 1975.

73. Goetz, E. M., and Baer, D. M. "Social Control of Form Diversity and the Emergence of New Forms in Childrens' Blockbuilding." *Journal of Applied Behavior Analysis* 6:209–17; 1973.

74. Goldstein, J. "Organize those Swim Sessions." *The Athletic Journal* 53:19, 71; November 1972.

75. Graham, G. M. "A Bridge Between 'What Is' and 'What Could Be.' " *The Physical Educator* 32:14–16; March 1975.

76. Grandgenett, R. "Individualizing PE in the Primary Grades." *Journal of Health, Physical Education, and Recreation* 46:51; February 1976.

77. Hall, R. V. *The Measurement of Behavior.* Lawrence, Kans.: H & H Enterprises (P. O. Box 3342), 1971. 37 pp.

78. ———. *Behavior Modification: Applications in School and Home.* Lawrence, Kans.: H & H Enterprises (P. O. Box 3342), 1971. 59 pp.

79. ———, and Broden, M. "Behavior Changes in Brain-Injured Children Through Social Reinforcement." *Journal of Experimental Child Psychology* 5:463–79; 1967.

80. ———, and others. "Teachers and Parents as Researchers Using

Multiple Baseline Designs." *Journal of Applied Behavior Analysis* 3:247–55; 1970.

81. _____; Lund, D.; and Jackson, D. "Effects of Teacher Attention on Study Behavior." *Journal of Applied Behavior Analysis* 1:1–12; 1968.

82. Hammond, M. "Motivating those #4 and #5 Men." *Scholastic Coach* 43:28; March 1974.

83. Harris, F. R., and others. "Effects of Positive Social Reinforcement on Regressed Crawling of a Nursery School Child." *Journal of Educational Psychology* 55:35–41; 1964.

84. Hasazi, J. B., and Hasazi, S. E. "Effects of Teacher Attention on Digit-Reversal Behavior in an Elementary Schoolchild." *Journal of Applied Behavior Analysis* 5:157–62; 1972.

85. Haughton, E. "Myriad Counter (or, Beads that Aren't for Worrying). *Teaching Exceptional Children* 6:203–209; 1974.

86. Hayes, L. A. "The Use of Group Contingencies for Behavioral Control: A Review." *Psychological Bulletin* 83:628–48.

87. Hoffman, S. J. "Traditional Methodology: Prospects for Change." *Quest* 15:51–59; 1971.

88. Homme, L. E., and others. *How to Use Contingency Contracting in the Classroom.* Champaign, Ill.: Research Press, 1969. 130 pp.

89. Horner, R. D. "Establishing Use of Crutches by a Mentally Retarded Spina Bifida Child." *Journal of Applied Behavior Analysis* 4:183–89; 1971.

90. Howell, M. L. "Use of Force-Time Graphs for Performance Analysis in Facilitating Motor Learning." *Research Quarterly* 27:12–22; 1956.

91. Huffman, T. "Incentive Awards for Baseball." *The Athletic Journal* 52:84; March 1972.

92. Hughes, S. "Motivating the Below Average Swimmer." *The Athletic Journal* 54:74; February 1974.

93. Hunsicker, P. *Physical Fitness.* Wash., D. C.: National Education Association, 1963. 32 pp.

94. Jackson, D. A.; Mayville, W. J.; and Cowart, J. B., Jr. "The Auto-Pedestrian Safety Project." *Behavior Analysis and Education—1972.* (Edited by G. Semb.) Lawrence: Univ. of Kansas, Dept. of Human Development, 1972. pp. 310–17.

95. Johnson, B. L., and Nelson, J. K. *Practical Measurement for Evaluation in Physical Education.* Minneapolis: Burgess, 1974. 438 pp.

96. Johnson, S. M., and Lobitz, G. K. "The Personal and Marital Adjustment of Parents as Related to Observed Child Deviance and Parenting Behaviors." *Journal of Abnormal Child Psychology* 2:193–207; 1974.

97. Johnston, M. K., and others. "An Application of Reinforcement

Principles to Development of Motor Skills of a Young Child." *Child Development* 37:379–87; 1966.

98. Joslin, D. "Tennis Player Rating Index." *Coaching Clinic* 12:12–16; May 1974.

99. Katz, R. C., and Zlutnick, S., editors. *Behavior Therapy and Health Care: Principles and Applications.* New York: Pergamon, 1975. 624 pp.

100. Katzenberg, A. C. *How to Draw Graphs.* Kalamazoo, Mich.: Behaviordelia (P. O. Box 1044), 1975. 149 pp.

101. Kau, M. L., and Fisher, J. "Self-Modification of Exercise Behavior." *Journal of Behavior Therapy and Experimental Psychiatry* 5:213–14; 1974.

102. Kaye, R. A. "The Use of Waist-Type Flotation Device as an Adjunct in Teaching Beginning Swimming Skills." *Research Quarterly* 36:277–81; 1965.

103. Kazdin, A. E. "Response Cost—The Removal of Conditioned Reinforcers for Therapeutic Change." *Behavior Therapy* 3:533–46; 1972.

104. ———. "The Effect of Vicarious Reinforcement on Attentive Behavior in the Classroom." *Journal of Applied Behavior Analysis* 6:71–78; 1973.

105. ———. "Self-Monitoring and Behavior Change." *Self-Control: Power to the People.* (Edited by M. Mahoney and C. Thoreson.) Monterey, Calif.: Brooks/Cole, 1974. pp. 218–46.

106. ———. *Behavior Modification in Applied Settings.* Homewood, Ill.: Dorsey, 1975. 292 pp.

107. ———, and Kock, J. "The Effect of Nonverbal Approval on Student Attentive Behavior." *Journal of Applied Behavior Analysis* 6:643–54; 1973.

108. Kidd, F. M., and others. "Guidelines for Secondary School Physical Education." *Journal of Health Physical Education and Recreation* 42:47–50; April 1971.

109. Kleinknecht, R. A. "A Program of Behavior Modification for Problem Drivers." *Advances in Behavior Therapy, 1968.* (Edited by R. D. Rubin and C. M. Franks.) New York: Academic Press, 1969. pp. 211–19.

110. Knapczyk, D. R., and Yoppi, J. O. "Development of Cooperative and Competitive Play Responses in Developmentally Disabled Children." *American Journal of Mental Deficiency* 80:245–55; 1975.

111. Knapp, M. E.; O'Neil, S. M.; and Allen, K. E. "Teaching Suzi to Walk by Behavior Modification of Motor Skills." *Nursing Forum* 13:159–83; 1974.

112. Knapp, T. J., and Shodahl, S. A. "Ben Franklin as a Behavior Modifier: A Note." *Behavior Therapy* 5:656–60; 1974.
113. Kozloff, M. A. *Reaching the Autistic Child: A Parent Training Program.* Champaign, Ill.: Research Press, 1973. 245 pp.
114. Kubany, E. S. "65 Ways to Say 'Good for You.' " *Teacher* 90:47; September 1972.
115. Kunzelmann, H. P., editor. *Precision Teaching: An Initial Training Sequence.* Seattle, Wash.: Special Child Publications, 1970. 310 pp.
116. Kuypers, D. S.; Becker, W. C.; and O'Leary, K. D. "How to Make a Token System Fail." *Exceptional Children* 35:101–09; 1968.
117. Larche, H. E., and Larche, D. W. "Success and Excellence in Teaching: Reality Therapy for Physical Education." *The Physical Educator* 32:194–98; December 1975.
118. Laughlin, N. T. "Positive Motivation in Coaching." *Scholastic Coach* 66:124–25; May/June 1975.
119. Leat, C. A. M. "Promoting Parents' Interest in Physical Education." *Journal of Health, Physical Education, and Recreation.* 44:85; November/December 1973.
120. Lebow, M. D. *Behavior Modification: A Significant Method in Nursing Practice.* Englewood Cliffs, N. J.: Prentice-Hall, 1973. 271 pp.
121. Leitenberg, H., editor. *Handbook of Behavior Modification and Behavior Therapy.* Englewood Cliffs, N. J.: Prentice-Hall, 1976. 671 pp.
122. Lewis, S. "A Comparison of Behavior Therapy Techniques in the Reduction of Fearful Avoidance Behavior." *Behavior Therapy* 5: 1974, 648–55.
123. Libb, J. W., and Clements, C. B. "Token Reinforcement in an Exercise Program for Hospitalized Geriatric Patients." *Perceptual and Motor Skills* 28:957–58; 1969.
124. Lindsley, O. R. "A Reliable Wrist Counter for Recording Behavior Rates." *Journal of Applied Behavior Analysis* 1:77–78; 1968.
125. Loeber, R., and Weisman, R. G. "Contingencies of Therapist and Trainer Performance: A Review." *Psychological Bulletin* 82:660–88; 1975.
126. Loviband, S. H. "Use of Behavior Modification in the Reduction of Alcohol Related Road Accidents." *Applications of Behavior Modification.* (Edited by T. Thompson and W. S. Dockens, III) New York: Academic Press, 1975. pp. 399–406.
127. Lovitt, T. C., and Curtiss, K. A. "Academic Response Rate as a Function of Teacher- and Self-Imposed Contingencies." *Journal of Applied Behavior Analysis* 2:49–53; 1969.
128. Luthans, F., and Kreitner, R. *Organizational Behavior Modification.* Glenview, Ill.: Scott, Foresman & Co., 1975. 214 pp.
129. MacDonald, M. L., and Butler, A. K. "Reversal of Helplessness:

Producing Walking Behavior in Nursing Home Wheelchair Residents Using Behavior Modification Procedures. *Journal of Gerentology* 29:97–101; 1974.

130. Madsen, C. H., Jr.; Becker, W. C.; and Thomas, D. R. "Rules, Praise, and Ignoring: Elements of Elementary Classroom Control." *Journal of Applied Behavior Analysis* 1:139–50; 1968.

131. ———; and others. "An Analysis of the Reinforcing Function of 'Sit-Down' Commands." *Readings in Educational Psychology.* (Edited by R. K. Parker.) Boston: Allyn and Bacon, 1968. pp. 265–78.

132. ———, and Madsen, C. K. *Teaching/Discipline: A Positive Approach for Educational Development.* Boston: Allyn and Bacon, 1974. 265 pp.

133. ———, and others. "Classroom RAID (Rules, Approval, Ignore, Disapproval): A Cooperative Approach for Professionals and Volunteers." *Journal of School Psychology* 8:180–85; 1970.

134. Mager, R. F. *Preparing Instructional Objectives.* Palo Alto, Calif.: Fearon, 1962. 60 pp.

135. Mahoney, K. "Count on it: A Simple Self-Monitoring Device." *Behavior Therapy* 5:701–703; 1974.

136. Mahoney, M. J. "Research Issues in Self-Management." *Behavior Therapy* 3:45–63; 1972.

137. Maletzky, B. M. "Behavior Recording as Treatment: A Brief Note." *Behavior Therapy* 5:107–11; 1974.

138. Malina, R. M. "Effects of Varied Information Feedback Conditions on Throwing Speed and Accuracy." *Research Quarterly* 40:134–45; 1969.

139. Mandelker, A. V.; Brigham, T. A.; and Bushell, D., Jr. "The Effects of Token Procedures on a Teacher's Social Contacts with Her Students." *Journal of Applied Behavior Analysis* 3:169–74; 1970.

140. Mariani, T. "A Comparison of the Command Method and the Task Method of Teaching the Forehand and Backhand Tennis Strokes." *Research Quarterly* 41:171–74; 1970.

141. Masche, K. A. "Effects of Two Different Programs of Instruction on Motor Performance of Second Grade Students." *Research Quarterly* 41:406–11; 1970.

142. Mash, E. J.; Handy, L. E.; and Hammerlynck, L. A., editors. *Behavior Modification Approaches to Parenting.* New York: Brunner/Mazel, 1976. 254 pp.

143. Mattos, R. L. "A Manual Counter for Recording Multiple Behavior." *Journal of Applied Behavior Analysis* 1:130; 1968.

144. McAllister, L. W., and others. "The Application of Operant Conditioning Techniques in a Secondary School Classroom." *Journal of Applied Behavior Analysis* 2:277–85; 1969.

145. McClannahan, L. E., and Risley, T. R. "Design of Living Environ-

ments for Nursing-Home Residents: Increasing Participation in Recreation Activities." *Journal of Applied Behavior Analysis* 8:261–68; 1975.

146. McCord, J. D. B. "Chart the Pitchers." *The Athletic Journal* 53:86, 88–89; March 1973.

147. McDonald, L. J. "An Elective Curriculum: Day-to-Day Choices." *Journal of Health, Physical Education, and Recreation* 42:28–29; September 1971.

148. McFadden, J. "Motivating Team Scoring in Cross-Country." *Scholastic Coach* 43:52, 74; February 1974.

149. McKenzie, T. L., and Rushall, B. S. "Effects of Self-Recording on Attendance and Performance in a Competitive Swimming Training Environment." *Journal of Applied Behavior Analysis* 7:199–206; 1974.

150. Meyerson, E.; Kerr, N.; and Michael, J. L. "Behavior Modification in Rehabilitation." *Child Development: Readings in Experimental Analysis* (Edited by S. W. Bijou and D. M. Baer.) N.Y.: Appleton-Century-Crofts, 1967. pp. 214–39.

151. Miller, L. K. *Everyday Behavior Analysis.* Monterey, Calif.: Brooks/Cole, 1976. 310 pp.

152. Morris, J. "A Handbook for Baseball Players." *Coaching Clinic* 11:2–4; November 1973.

153. Moser, D. L. "Good Discipline Is a Product of Good Teaching." *Journal of Health, Physical Education, and Recreation* 42:23; June 1971.

154. Mudra, D. "A Perceptual Approach to Winning: The Coach and the Learning Process." *Journal of Health, Physical Education, and Recreation* 41:26–29, 56; May 1970.

155. ———. "Personality Tests: Panacea or Phantasy." *Scholastic Coach* 43:20, 22, 97; May 1974.

156. Neisworth, J. T., and Smith, R. M. *Modifying Retarded Behavior.* Boston: Houghton Mifflin, 1973. 220 pp.

157. Nixon, J. E., and Locke, L. F. "Research on Teaching Physical Education." *Second Handbook of Research on Teaching.* (Edited by R. M. W. Travers.) Chicago: Rand-McNally, 1973. pp. 1210–42.

158. Nolan, J. D. "The True Humanist: The Behavior Modifier." *The Teachers College Record* 76:335–43; 1974.

159. Nygaard, G. "Interaction Analysis of Physical Education Classes." *Research Quarterly* 46:351–57; 1975.

160. O'Brian, F., and Azrin, N. H. "Behavioral Engineering: Control of Posture by Informational Feedback." *Journal of Applied Behavior Analysis* 3:235–40; 1970.

161. ———; ———; and Bugle, C. "Training Profoundly Retarded

Children to Stop Crawling." *Journal of Applied Behavior Analysis* 5:131–37; 1972.

162. O'Leary, K. D. "Behavior Modification in the Classroom: A Rejoinder to Winett and Winkler." *Journal of Applied Behavior Analysis* 5:505–11; 1972.

163. ———, and Drabman, R. "Token Reinforcement Programs in the Classroom: A Review." *Psychological Bulletin* 75:379–98; 1971.

164. ———, and others. "The Effects of Loud and Soft Reprimands on the Behavior of Disruptive Students." *Exceptional Children* 37:145–55; 1970.

165. ———, Poulos, R. W.; and Devine, V. T. "Tangible Reinforcers: Bonuses or Bribes?" *Journal of Consulting and Clinical Psychology* 38:1–8; 1972.

166. ———, and Wilson, G. T. *Behavior Therapy: Application and Outcome.* Englewood Cliffs, N.J.: Prentice-Hall, 1975. 496 pp.

167. Panyan, M. C. *Behavior Modification: New Ways to Teach New Skills.* Lawrence, Kans.: H & H Enterprises (P. O. Box 3342), 1972. 32 pp.

168. Pecor, B. "Interesting Cross-Country Practice." *The Athletic Journal* 54:26, 45; June 1974.

169. Pelton, B. C. "A Critical Analysis of Current Practices and Beliefs Underlying General Physical Education Programs in Higher Education." *Research Quarterly* 68:678–85; 1967.

170. ———. "Research Directed for the Twenty-First Century." *The Physical Educator* 33:34–38; March 1976.

171. Peterson, R. A. and McIntosh, E. I. "Teaching Tricycle Riding." *Mental Retardation* 5:32–34; October 1973.

172. Pierce, C. H., and Risley, T. R. "Improving Job Performance of Neighborhood Youth Corps Aides in an Urban Recreation Program." *Journal of Applied Behavior Analysis* 7:207–15; 1974.

173. ———, and ———. "Recreation as a Reinforcer: Increasing Membership and Decreasing Disruptions in an Urban Recreation Center." *Journal of Applied Behavior Analysis* 7:403–11; 1974.

174. Pietrangeli, N. "Developing the 'Thinking Wrestler.' " *Coaching Clinic* 11:10–13; September 1973.

175. Polidoro, J. R. "Performance Objectives: A Practical Approach Toward Accountability." *The Physical Educator* 33:20–23; March 1976.

176. Pomerleau, O.; Bass, F.; and Crown, V. "Role of Behavior Modification in Preventive Medicine." *New England Journal of Medicine* 292 (No. 24):1277–82; 1975.

177. Posner, M. I., and Keele, S. W. "Skill Learning." *Second Handbook of*

Research on Teaching. (Edited by R. M. W. Travers.) Chicago: Rand-McNally, 1973. pp. 805–31.

178. Presbie, R. J., and Brown, P. L. *Behavior Modification.* Wash., D. C.: National Education Association, 1976. 36 pp.

179. Quilitch, H. R. "A Portable, Programmed, Audible Timer." *Journal of Applied Behavior Analysis* 5:18; 1972.

180. Ramp, E., and Semb, G., editors. *Behavior Analysis: Areas of Research and Application.* Englewood Cliffs, N.J.: Prentice-Hall, 1973. 417 pp.

181. Raw, J., and Errickson, E. "Behavior Modification in Therapeutic Recreation." *Behavior Modification of the Mentally Retarded.* (Edited by T. Thompson, and J. Grabowski.) New York: Oxford Univ. Press, 1972. pp. 237–50.

182. Rickard, H. C., and Dinoff, M., editors. *Behavior Modification in Children: Case Studies and Illustrations from a Summer Camp.* Tuscaloosa: Univ. of Alabama Press, 1974. 174 pp.

183. Ritschl, C.; Mongrella, J.; and Presbie, R. J. "Group Time-Out from Rock and Roll Music and Out-of-Seat Behavior of Handicapped Children While Riding a School Bus." *Psychological Reports* 31:967–73; 1972.

184. Roundy, E. S. "Problems of and Competencies Needed by Men Physical Education Teachers at the Secondary Level." *Research Quarterly* 38:274–82; 1967.

185. Rushall, B. S. "Personality Profiles and a Theory of Behavior Modification for Swimmers." *Swimming Technique* 4:66–71, 76; 1967.

186. ———. "Some Applications of Psychology to Swimming." *Swimming Technique* 7:71–82; 1970.

187. ———. "Behaviour Control in Swimming." *The Australian Journal of Sports Medicine* 4:18–19, 22–24; April 1972.

188. ———, and Pettinger, J. "An Evaluation of the Effect of Various Reinforcers used as Motivators in Swimming." *Research Quarterly* 40:540–45; 1969.

189. ———, and Siedentop, D. *The Development and Control of Behavior in Sport and Physical Education.* Philadelphia: Lea and Febiger, 1972. 238 pp.

190. Sachs, D. A. "Behavioral Techniques in a Residential Nursing Home Facility." *Journal of Behavior Therapy and Experimental Psychiatry* 6:123–27; 1975.

191. Sand, P. L., and others. "Behavior Modification in the Medical Rehabilitation Setting: Rational and Some Applications." *Rehabilitation Research and Practice Review* 1:11–24; 1970.

192. Sanders, R. M., and Hanson, P. J. "A Note on a Simple Procedure

for Redistributing a Teacher's Student Contacts." *Journal of Applied Behavior Analysis* 4:157–61; 1971.

193. ———; Hopkins, B. L.; and Walker, M. B. "An Inexpensive Method for Making Data Records of Complex Behaviors." *Journal of Applied Behavior Analysis* 2:221–22; 1969.

194. ———, and Paine, F. "Time Lapse Automation." *Journal of Applied Behavior Analysis* 5:110; 1972.

195. Schaefer, H. H., and Martin, P. L. *Behavioral Therapy.* New York: McGraw-Hill, 1975. 378 pp.

196. Schlitz, J. W. "Let Them See How They Swim!" *Scholastic Coach* 42:38, 40; January 1973.

197. Schwartz, F. "Use of Positive Reinforcement to Attain Proper Walking in a Severely Retarded Child." *School Application of Learning Theory* 5 (No. 2):31–38; 1973.

198. Schwartz, S. "A Learning-Based System to Categorize Teacher Behavior." *Quest* 17:52–55; 1972.

199. Schwitzgebel, R. L., and Schwitzgebel, R. K., editors. *Psychotechnology: Electronic Control of the Mind.* New York: Holt, Rinehart and Winston, 1973. 341 pp.

200. Scoles, G. "Take the Guesswork out of Weight Training." *Scholastic Coach* 42:51, 58; December 1972.

201. Screven, C. G. "Research on Running Time and Physical Work of Children Under Various Reinforcement Conditions." *Child Development* 30:461–69; 1959.

202. Seaton, D. C., and others. *Physical Education Handbook.* Englewood Cliffs, N.J.: Prentice-Hall, 1974. 442 pp.

203. Serino, K. "The Effects of Monetary Reinforcement on the Number of Exercises Done Nightly." Unpublished manuscript. New Paltz, N. Y.: State University of New York, Psychology Department, 1976.

204. Sherman, A. R. "Real-Life Exposure as a Primary Therapeutic Factor in the Desensitization Treatment of Fear." *Journal of Abnormal Psychology* 79:19–28; 1972.

205. Shockely, J. M., Jr. "Needed: Behavioral Objectives in Physical Education." *Journal of Health, Physical Education, and Recreation* 44:44–46; April 1973.

206. Siedentop, D. "Behavior Analysis and Teacher Training." *Quest* 18:26–32; 1972.

207. ———. "On Tilting at Windmills while Rome Burns." *Quest* 18:94–97; 1972.

208. ———, and Rushall, B. "An Operant Model for Skill Acquisition." *Quest* 17:82–90; 1972.

209. Simonian, C. "Fencing: Keep it Simple!" *Scholastic Coach* 43:58, 60; December 1973.

210. Singer, R. N. "Transfer Effects and Ultimate Success in Archery Due to Degree of Difficulty of the Initial Learning." *Research Quarterly* 37:532–39; 1966.

211. ———. "A Systems Approach to Teaching Physical Education." *Journal of Health, Physical Education, and Recreation* 45:33–36, 86; September 1974.

212. ———. *Motor Learning and Human Performance: An Application to Physical Education Skills.* New York: Macmillan, 1975. 549 pp.

213. Skinner, B. F. "What Is the Experimental Analysis of Behavior?" *Journal of the Experimental Analysis of Behavior* 9:213–18; 1966.

214. Sloat, K. S. M., and Loganbill, L. "A Medium-Cost, High-Quality 'Bug-in-the-Ear' System." *Behavior Therapy* 7:409–10; 1976.

215. Smith, C. D. "Help Them Turn On Positively." *Journal of Health, Physical Education, and Recreation* 45:27–28; June 1974.

216. Spasoff, T. "Let's Have More Applied Research." *Journal of Health, Physical Education, and Recreation* 45:24; June 1974.

217. Starcher, R. W. "Analysis of Offensive Efficiency." *The Athletic Journal* 53:50, 73; January 1973.

218. Stevens, G. "Use Incentives for Motivation." *The Athletic Journal* 54:72–73; May 1974.

219. Striefel, S. *Behavior Modification: Teaching a Child to Imitate.* Lawrence, Kans.: H & H Enterprises (P. O. Box 3342), 1974. 49 pp.

220. Stuart, R. B., and Davis, B. *Slim Chance in a Fat World: Behavioral Control of Obesity.* Condensed edition. Champaign, Ill.: Research Press, 1972. 104 pp.

221. Strunkard, A. J. "Presidential Address—1974: From Explanation to Action in Psychosomatic Medicine: The Case of Obesity." *Psychosomatic Medicine* 37:195–236; 1975.

222. ———, and Mahoney, M. J. "Behavioral Treatment of the Eating Disorders." *Handbook of Behavior Modification and Behavior Therapy.* (Edited by H. Leitenberg.) Englewood Cliffs, N. J.: Prentice-Hall, 1976. pp. 45–73.

223. Stumphauzer, J. S., editor. *Behavior Therapy with Delinquents.* Springfield, Ill.: C. C. Thomas, 1973. 358 pp.

224. Taylor, P. A. "Altering the Amount of Walking Behavior by means of a Punishment Contingency." Unpublished manuscript. New York: Pace University, Psychology Department, 1976.

225. Thomas, E. J., editor. *Behavior Modification Procedure: A Sourcebook.* Chicago: Aldine, 1974. 322 pp.

226. Thomas, D. R.; Becker, W. C.; and Armstrong, M. "Production and

Elimination of Disruptive Classroom Behavior by Systematically Varying Teacher's Behavior." *Journal of Applied Behavior Analysis* 1:35–45; 1968.

227. Thompson, D. H. "Immediate External Feedback in the Learning of Golf Skills." *Research Quarterly* 40:589–94; 1969.

228. Thompson, T., and Dockens, W. S., III, editors. *Applications of Behavior Modification.* New York: Academic Press, 1975. 540 pp.

229. ———, and Grabowski, J., editors. *Behavior Modification of the Mentally Retarded.* New York: Oxford Univ. Press, 1972. 297 pp.

230. Thoresen, C. E., editor. *Behavior Modification in Education: The Seventy-Second Yearbook of the National Society for the Study of Education. Part 1.* Chicago: Univ. of Chicago Press, 1973. 474 pp.

231. Thoresen, C. E., and Mahoney, M. J. *Behavioral Self-Control.* New York: Holt, Rinehart and Winston, 1974. 177 pp.

232. Tiedemann, R. "Psychological Factors of Coaching." *Coaching Clinic* 14:13–15; February 1975.

233. Travers, R. M. W., editor. *Second Handbook of Research on Teaching.* Chicago: Rand-McNally, 1973. 1400 pp.

234. Van Houten, R. V., and Sullivan, K. "Effects of an Audio Cueing System on the Rate of Teacher Praise." *Journal of Applied Behavior Analysis* 8:197–201; 1975.

235. Vannier, M.; Foster, M.; and Gallahue, D. L. *Teaching Physical Education in Elementary Schools.* Philadelphia: W. B. Saunders, 1973. 702 pp.

236. Violette, H. "High School Golf: Keep It Simple." *Coaching Clinic* 12:9–10; January 1974.

237. Wahler, R. G. "Setting Generality: Some Specific and General Effects of Child Behavior Therapy." *Journal of Applied Behavior Analysis* 2:239–46; 1969.

238. ———, and Cormier, W. H. "The Ecological Interview: A First Step in Out-Patient Child Behavior Therapy." *Journal of Behavior Therapy and Experimental Psychiatry* 1:279–89; 1970.

239. Walker, H. M., and Buckley, N. K. *Token Reinforcement Techniques: Classroom Applications for the Hard-to-Teach Child.* Eugene, Oregon: E-B Press (1410 Orchard St.) 1974. 225 pp.

240. Warren, S. A. "To What Behaviors Do Attending Adults Respond?" *American Journal of Mental Deficiency* 75:449–55; 1971.

241. Watson, D. L., and Tharp, R. G. *Self-Directed Behavior: Self-Modification for Personal Adjustment.* Monterey, Calif.: Brooks/Cole, 1972. 264 pp.

242. Watson, L. S., Jr. *How to Use Behavior Modification with Mentally Retarded and Autistic Children: Programs for Administrators, Teachers, Parents and Nurses.* Tuscaloosa, Alabama: Behavior Modification Technology (81 Arcadia Drive), 1972. 237 pp.

243. _____. *Child Behavior Modification. A Manual for Teachers, Nurses, and Parents.* New York: Pergamon, 1973. 147 pp.

244. Wheeler, A. H., and Fox, W. L. *A Teacher's Guide to Writing Instructional Objectives.* Lawrence, Kans.: H & H Enterprises, (P.O. Box 3342), 1972. 39 pp.

245. White, M. A. "Natural Rates of Teacher Approval and Disapproval in the Classroom." *Journal of Applied Behavior Analysis* 8:367–72.

246. Williams, R. L., and Long, J. D. *Toward a Self-Managed Life Style.* Boston: Houghton Mifflin, 1975. 235 pp.

247. Wills, T. A.; Weiss, R. L.; and Patterson, G. R. "A Behavioral Analysis of the Determinants of Marital Satisfaction." *Journal of Consulting and Clinical Psychology* 42:802–11; 1974.

248. Wilson, S.; Buzzell, N.; and Jensen, M. "Observational Research: A Practical Tool." *The Physical Educator* 32:90–93; 1975.

249. Winett, R. A., and Winkler, R. C. "Current Behavior Modification in the Classroom: Be Still, Be Quiet, Be Docile." *Journal of Applied Behavior Analysis* 5:499–504; 1972.

250. Wright, E. J. "Effects of Light and Heavy Equipment on Acquisition of Sports-Type Skills by Young Children." *Research Quarterly* 38:705–14; 1967.

251. Yen, S., and McIntire, R. W., editors. *Teaching Behavior Modification.* Kalamazoo, Mich.: Behaviordelia (P. O. Box 1044), 1976. 264 pp.